THE POOR
YOU HAVE WITH YOU ALWAYS

THE POOR
YOU HAVE WITH YOU ALWAYS

Alan Keith–Lucas

ISBN 0-9623634-0-5

CONTENTS

FOREWORD

Alan Keith-Lucas is probably best known throughout the social work profession as the author of *Giving and Taking Help*, a practice treatise which is remarkable for its simplicity and depth. Nevertheless, his written works are quite wide-ranging, including numerous articles and books concerning child welfare, church social work, public social services, and social work philosophy.

But Keith (as he is known to colleagues and friends across the country and around the world) is more than an able writer. He is a skillful practitioner, a competent administrator, an articulate speaker, a beloved teacher, a renowned storyteller, a sought-after consultant, and a longstanding member of the North American Association of Christians in Social Work and a valued member of its Board of Directors.

The present book has been ably edited by David A. Sherwood, also a member of the Board of Directors of NACSW and the current Editor of its journal, *Social Work and Christianity*.

I am pleased to commend this work to the social work profession and to all who are committed to the well-being of people.

Edward G. Kuhlmann
Executive Director
North American Association of
Christians in Social Work

Preface

In this book I have attempted to bring together into one coherent history what people have thought and done about the problem of poverty throughout Western, and more particularly, British and American civilization.

I have not been concerned to any great extent with the discovery of new and unfamiliar data and have relied largely on the scholarship and the discrimination of such authors as de Schweinitz, Troeltsch, Uhlhorn, and Pumphrey and Pumphrey.

The first part of this book owes its origin to research I did as a participant in a seminar, under a grant from the Lilly foundation, in Politics and Religion, at Duke University in the summer of 1958. My thanks are due to the Foundation and also to Dr. John H. Hallowell who both encouraged me and helped me to consider political theory in theological terms. The documentation style I used at the time did not include the name of the publishers and I have chosen to retain that style.

In a few cases, where the original was unavailable or the subject of the work had little to do with the problem I was considering, I have repeated quotations these writers saw as significant. In others, a quotation has led me back to the original work. These authors also reproduce, or excerpt at considerable length, documents or articles from the past. I have therefore distinguished in my references whether a statement is quoted directly from the original or from a piece reproduced or excerpted at length by another author, or is, as it were, a second-hand quote selected by the author in question. My interest has been, however, more in how a statement reflects the thought of the time than in presenting new material.

Alan Keith–Lucas
Chapel Hill
February 1989

Foundations: Moses to the Renaissance

The Problem

Care for the Poor

"The poor shall not cease out of the land," said the writer of Deuteronomy[1]. Every Western society has had within it people who cannot or do not support themselves and are dependent on others for help. While no accurate count can be made since definitions of poverty vary as well as what might be termed "help," probably the proportion of adults dependent on others has never fallen below five percent. At times it has been much higher, as for instance in the latter days of the Roman Empire, and it is at present probably not much higher or lower than the average over the years. Societies have from time to time launched campaigns to eliminate poverty, the most recent being Lyndon Johnson's "War on Poverty" in the 1960s. Although small gains may be made, the problem persists. Nor, as far as I am aware, has the problem ever been reduced to what might be thought of as its irreducible minimum: the handicapped, the sick, and the victims of identifiable disaster. There have always been apparently able-bodied poor as well as those whose incapacity is obvious.

Motives and Principles versus Causes and Mechanisms

This book is an attempt to trace the motives and principles of those who have tried, over the centuries, to help, support, and sometimes to control or reform this unassimilated group in society. It is not an attempt to explain why the poor are poor. The causes of poverty are only relevant to this study in that at any time or in the view of certain people what is perceived as the cause of poverty affects how the poor are treated.

There have been theological explanations. Ambrose thought that inequalities in possessions were a result of the Fall.[2] Chrysostom believed that God permitted poverty so that the well-to-do would have someone to give to, and therefore earn their reward in Heaven.[3] The Puritans, at least some of them, held that the poor were the non-elect who were deemed an insult to God.[4]

Most common, historically, have been moral explanations. The poor have consistently been accused of laziness and intemperance. John Locke, the philosopher of liberty, wrote in 1696 that the increase of the poor could only be caused by "the relaxation of discipline and the corruption of manners."[5] By equating lack of election with lack of belief, poverty has been seen as both a result of vice and of failure to do God's will. This is at least implied by a statement attributed to the Reverend Jerry Falwell to the effect that material wealth is God's way of rewarding those who do his will, and, presumably, poverty His way of punishing those who don't.[6] Lack of thrift has often been charged to the poor. One Victorian clergyman opposed any form of financial assistance to the aged as inimical to God's ordinance in favor of thrift.[7] Thomas Addams held that God allows particular people to be poor because they would not be able to withstand the temptations that go with wealth, thus combining morality and theology in a novel way.[8]

Sometimes the "deserving poor" have been excused these judgments, as in Bishop Ridley's sixteenth century categorization of the poor as "the poore by impotencie, the poore by casualtie and the thriftles poore," but often they have been lumped together as a class, perhaps under the assumption that impotency and casualty are signs of God's displeasure. Thus, we find a British writer in 1889 holding that "kindness to an individual too often means cruelty to a class,"[9] and an American report of about that time listing the causes of poverty as primarily intemperance, but also old age, sickness, being crippled, misfortune in business, insanity, idiocy, blindness, deafness, orphanage, desertion, and (with no sense of having changed direction) ignorance, improvidence, vicious habits, thriftlessness, laziness, and bad management.[10] Just occasionally, the moral onus rests on the well-do-do, who are seen as exploiting the poor, as in most early twentieth century "social hymns," such as Walter Russell Bowie's "Holy City Seen of John" and Frank North's "Where Cross the Crowded Ways of Life," both of which speak of greed, although the latter also speaks of "haunts of wretchedness and need." But these are exceptions to the general rule.

There are also sociological and economic explanations, ranging from the effects of the Enclosure Acts to technological unemployment and economic maladjustments, such as the great depression of the 1930s, and disasters such as the potato famine in Ireland in the 1840s and the Black Death in the 14th Century. Whether one should include among these Thomas Chalmer's belief that poverty could be abolished if the poor should only limit their procreative impulses, which he sees as "irrefragable as the most rigid demonstration"[11] (the word "proletariat," after all, means the class that breeds) is questionable. Although a sociological factor, procreation is supposed to be under the control of the poor themselves and their failure to take the necessary action may be considered the result

2

of either concupiscence or ignorance. In the twentieth century there has also been some recognition that an economic system that favors the majority of the people may at the same time leave part of the population poor, so that the battle against inflation may increase unemployment or a free market depress wages.

But these theories are only significant for our purposes as people come to believe in them. Nor will this book describe in detail the various mechanisms and institutions humankind has devised to cope with the poor. There are two reasons for this. First, there are many accounts of these programs and mechanisms, the best of which are probably Karl de Schweinitz' *England's Road to Social Security* and Sophonisba Breckinridge's *Public Welfare Administration in the United States: Selected Documents*, to both of which I owe a tremendous debt and many illustrations of the principles employed. And second, these programs, mechanisms, and institutions, as well as the laws under which they were developed, are reflections of the motives and principles which are the subject of this book.

Suffice it to say that in the course of the history we are dealing with here – in general the history of Western civilization from Biblical times to the present day – society has used at least the following mechanisms: the commune, the hospice, exhortation to private givers, the allocation of the tithe, settlement laws, overseers of the poor, the means test, the workhouse, subsidization of wages, work-relief, less-eligibility, social insurance, public assistance as an enforceable right, public provision of certain benefits such as education or health care, graduated taxation (although a negative income tax has been suggested I do not believe that it has been actualized anywhere), the distribution of surplus commodities, soup kitchens, guilds, mutual aid societies, and demogrants.

Diversion and Change of Direction: Apostacy and Revival

There is also the problem that these programs may start with one set of ideals and gradually become diverted from their original direction without changing too much in form. This is certainly what has happened to Aid to Families with Dependent Children in the United States. It was originally conceived as a a long-time income replacement program, strictly financial and enabling single parents to stay at home with their children. It very soon began to accumulate rehabilitative overtones, to demand that the single parent work, if at all possible, and to urge recipients to exert every effort to become self-supporting as soon as they could.[12]

This theme of a gradual change in direction or meaning in all human institutions, and indeed in any principle or motive, while maintaining

3

similar form or language, is one that is central to this book. England's road, and America's, is not a straight uphill progression. Where there has been progress this has often taken place in a dialectic process: thesis, antithesis, and synthesis. Or, if one prefers a different image, it happens by swings of the pendulum from one extreme to the other. But the synthesis or the coming back to the more moderate position has not always meant progress, which, for the purposes of this book, is defined as a more humane, dignity-enhancing or compassionate way of dealing with the problem. We have an almost infinite ability to pervert our institutions and stated principles. Thus, representative government can become rule by special interest groups, love decline into indulgence, liberty to license, patriotism to jingoism, and a moral right to a selfish demand for preferential treatment. A realistic model of what has happened is not a generally upward line, with perhaps a plateau or two on the way, thus:

or even a series of hills and valleys, the hills more or less overcoming the valleys, thus:

but a series of new starts and a wandering away from the direction of that start, each of which could be drawn something like this:

Progress, then, occurs only when a new idea is born, or when either a major happening (such as the Reformation, a World War, a great

Depression), or on a lesser scale, the "client revolt" of the 1960's, or some person or theory (the impact of Freud is a good example) forces people to reconsider their assumptions. There is then a return to the original direction and a new direction built on that, which might be diagrammed as below. This is the role played by the prophets in the Old Testament — to bring the people back to essentials: "What does the Lord require of you, but to do justice, to love kindness, and to walk humbly with your God."[13] Indeed, the Old Testament can be read as a paradigm of the process of this drift and revival process.

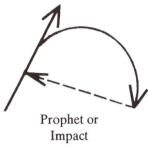

Prophet or
Impact

Lionel Trilling recognized this process in relation to our desire to help other people. Speaking of the moral passions which, he says," are even more willful and imperious and impatient than the self-seeking passions," he adds:

> we must be aware of the dangers which lie in our most generous wishes. Some paradox of our natures leads us, when once we have made our fellow men the objects of our enlightened interest, to go on to make them the objects of our pity, then of our wisdom, ultimately of our coercion.[14]

It is with this process in mind, and remembering Ranke's dictum that "every generation is equidistant from eternity"[15] that we will explore the impulse to help the poor and what has apparently happened to it.

The Impulse to Help

Why Help? Four Basic Principles

No one knows why human beings are willing to help those who cannot help themselves. There may have been human societies where the poor and the sick were simply left to starve or die of disease, and at times this has even been suggested, in theory at least, to be desirable, as in the works of the Social Darwinists and those who are afraid that by trying to feed the victims of famine we are only contributing to the "population explosion" and ensuring greater famine still. But the Golden Rule is as old as Hammurabi at least. The fear that one might oneself need help one day may be at the bottom of it. The sociobiologists would ascribe it to an instinct for the preservation of the species, but have some problem in explaining why certain species, whales for instance and perhaps elephants, do seem to care for the sick and the wounded, but other species clearly do not. The faithful believe that God commands it. Humanists believe that it is somehow characteristic of humankind as we have evolved as social creatures. With their more or less single-minded concentration on humankind and our welfare, the humanists have often put it at the top of their hierarchy of values, without giving too much attention to its roots.

What we do know is that there have been, in the course of Western history, four principles, or conscious motives, for helping the less fortunate. These can, somewhat simplistically, be assigned to three civilizations and one religious movement.

Hebrew Justice

From the Hebrew world came the idea of justice. This was basically a religious concept. It held that every human being, as a child of God, had the right to some small part of God's provenance. No person, or class of persons, had the right to take everything. The entire concept was wider than this. It included the use of just weights and measures and the prohibition against using one's superior status or power to take advantage of the poor; but the writer of Exodus commanded that fields not be gleaned "so that the poor may eat,"[16] which was what Boaz did for Naomi and Ruth. Proverbs praises the man "who knows the rights of the poor."[17] The word "rights" is significant: it establishes something which personal judgment cannot deny. Micah puts justice before kindness and so does the Old Testament as a whole. There are 105 references to justice in the Old Testament, 32 to compassion and 21 to kindness, and although these do not all refer to the poor, the poor were certainly included, often specifically. It is not surprising to find that many of the strongest advocates of a strictly "rights" program of public assistance have been Jewish or that in the nineteenth century Jewish writers were critical of Christian practice and the judgments it passed on the poor.[18]

Christian love

The Christian contribution, which arose out of the Jewish, and is foreshadowed at least in the book of Hosea, was that of love, or charity in its original meaning, which included the concept of valuing, thinking well of, its recipient.

The best description of it in its purest form is Paul's, in 1 Corinthians 13, with its emphasis on not insisting on its own way and its capacity to endure. Its mainspring is a response to love; the Christian felt that since he had been greatly loved he (or she) could do little else than love in turn. It also included two related concepts: the demand to love one's enemies as well as one's friends and Paul's statement that "there is now no distinction since all have fallen short of the glory of God."[19]

Self-Fulfillment and Responsibility

But Christianity early encountered both the Greek and the Roman world. From the Greek came the concept that persons were only self-fulfilled if they were involved with others, that the private person was an "idiot." Although this had largely to do with involvement in community affairs it also referred to the matter of helping those in distress. From the Roman world came the idea that the more fortunate had a responsibility, even a duty, toward the poor. This sense of "noblesse oblige" was practiced so assiduously in Rome that one writer calculates that in the later days of the Roman Empire there were 580,000 people receiving some sort of public subsidy and only 90,000 self-sufficient, a ratio of more than six to one,[20] and another that as early as the time of Julius Caesar there were 320,000 "annonae" (recipients of relief) in the city of Rome alone.[21] Those who are concerned with the size of the welfare rolls today might take note.

Diversion Again

These four principles—justice, charity, self-fulfillment, and responsibility—all arose from noble sentiments in the first place. All have to some extent been perverted. They have had to contend not only with human sin in the form of pride, selfishness, and insensitivity to the needs of others, but most of all to humanity's tendency to pass judgment on one another.

They have also had to compete with two other principles, in themselves basically good. One is the desire that one's actions should produce some moral good, and the other the need for order in society. These two principles, in turn, have been subject to the same kind of perversion as have our original four. The desire to do moral good can very easily become an excuse to control another person's actions and make her conform to one's own idea of goodness. At that point it invades both the concept of Christian charity and the sense of responsibility. It is a great temptation to pride and to considering the person one is helping as one's moral inferior. And since it involves a moral judgment it can strengthen our tendency to be judgmental and to decide that a person in need is not deserving of help.

The Need for Order

The need for order in society perhaps requires more documentation at this point, because it was such a strong force in the Middle Ages but was rarely brought into the argument directly, perhaps because it was simply assumed. It is, of course, not dead today. Uprisings of the poor and oppressed are seen as threats to stability and, in general, thought to be inspired by nations intent on destroying our present economic system. Luther was violently disapproving of the Peasants' Revolt of his time. An earlier one in England, with its motto "When Adam delved and Eve span, who was then the gentleman?" resulted in further repression. It is wise to recall that the Elizabethan Act of 1597 which established for the first time public responsibility for the poor was in fact an amendment to an Act of Henry VIII for the control of beggars and vagabonds.[22]

In its inception the need for order was based on the belief that God had ordained it. As a nineteenth century hymn put it, in a verse rarely sung today, "The rich man in his castle, the poor man at his gate / God made them, high or lowly, and ordered their estate."[23] Ambrose, as we have seen, may have ascribed economic inequities to the Fall, but most writers accepted society as it was and believed that it was ordained as such. This gave rise to belief in an absolute and unchangeable hierarchy, culminating in the Elizabethan "chain of being" which stretched from God, through archangels, angels, principalities and powers, to humanity in our various ranks, to beasts, plants, and even stones. So Shakespeare, when he writes of Anthony as a dolphin, is not comparing him to a fish but to the King of the Fishes. When Macbeth says, "Stand not upon the order of your going," he is signalizing the utter breakdown of an ordered society.[24]

The Directions of Diversion

But let us look at what has happened, at various times, to our original four principles.

Responsibility, which had clearly become perverted even while it was still principally Roman, can very easily become paternalism and colonialism — the "White Man's Burden" and the company town. It can become the justification for all sorts of intrusion into the lives of those for whom it assumes responsibility, in the name of "doing them good." It requires an elite, who may be either, in their own view, morally better or more knowledgable than the people they wish to help. It can be used to exercise social control. It is not perhaps merely coincidence that in the three most acclaimed extrapolations of our time, George Orwell's *1984*, Aldous Huxley's *Brave New World* and B. F. Skinner's *Walden Two*, it is the social scientist who carries out the program of those who control the population. Although in Skinner's case the control is seen as beneficial, inducing "right" behavior, it is nevertheless control and begs the question of whether the culture to which people are conformed is indeed a good one.

Self-fulfillment through helping others has been perverted in two directions. On the one hand it has often taken the form of a desire for gratitude, to be loved and thanked. On the other hand it may become the indulgence in pity, which is an emotion that always involves a belief in one's own superior fortune or kindness.[25] It can be seen today in the society man or woman who loves to visit children in Children's Homes and hand out goodies. It is essentially patronizing, and as such is relatively harmless except that it is not concerned with the real needs of the people it serves. It is also damaging to the recipient's self-respect, which means that it is probably not quite so harmless after all.

The peculiar quirk that self-fulfillment took, quite early in its history, came when self-fulfillment began to mean not a good feeling in this world, but salvation in the next. This was not confined to the ancient church, although it was perhaps its major heresy, but is clearly evident in some of the philanthropies of the great industrialists of the nineteenth and twentieth centuries, where it becomes a sort of eternal fire-insurance.

There are several variations on it. An Anglican Bishop in the eighteenth Century wrote, "Whatever is laid out in Charity, God accounts an Offering and a Loan to himself; and accordingly he engages to repay it."[26] Wesley gave it a moralistic tone. He remembered the camel and the eye of the needle:

> For religion must necessarily produce both industry and
> frugality and these cannot but produce riches. But as riches
> increase so will pride, anger and love of the world in all its
> branches . . . What way then can we take, that our money

may not sink us into the nethermost hell? There is one way and there is no other under heaven. If those who gain all they can, and save all they can, will likewise give all they can, the more they will grow in grace, and the more treasure they will lay up in Heaven.[27]

But probably the most callous statement, despite its apparent piety, is that of Sir Thomas Browne, author of the *Religio Medici:*

> I give no alms to satisfy the hunger of my brother, but to fulfill and accomplish the will and command of my God; I draw not my purse for his sake that demands it, but his that enjoined it; I relieve no man upon the rhetoric of his miseries, nor to content mine own commiserating disposition, for this is still but moral charity, and an act that oweth more to passion than reason.[28]

One might wonder what had happened to Matthew 25, where those who ministered to "the least of these" were surprised to find that they had been serving Jesus, or to the two halves of the Great Commandment: love God; love your neighbor as yourself.

Love

But the principle that suffered perhaps the greatest perversion was Christian love, or charity, as the debasement of that latter word testifies. The original impulse was apparently comparatively short-lived. It flourished for a while, as we know from the Book of Acts, and was sufficient to overcome distinctions of wealth, of citizenship, and of slave or free status. Despite present day criticism of Paul's alleged sexism, it greatly enhanced the status of women. Agapes, or love-feasts, persisted until the third century, when they were banned, having apparently gotten out of hand. But what was possible in the small closed community of the early church could not be carried out in the world at large and by the time of Constantine "the idea of equalizing social conditions for love's sake had entirely disappeared."[29]

Two other things had also happened to it. An early apochryphal gospel, perhaps relying on Paul's comment about free-loading at church suppers[30] puts into Jesus' mouth a denunciation of those "who hypocritically take" and "while they could help themselves, rather take alms from others."[31] Thus was manifested that particular devil, the fear that someone might receive something he did not deserve, which, although it has

10

plagued humanity ever since, seems to be more active in the United States than anywhere else.[32] It is perhaps worth noting that the question appears not to be emphasized in the Bible, although Paul reminds that the deliberately irresponsible should not be supported.[33] Both Jesus and Paul were most outspoken in their exhortations not to judge one's fellow man.[34]

Second, charity or love began to mean doing good by exhorting the poor to greater frugality, industry, or morality. Thus moral superiority was assumed, as in the following passage, which characteristically classes the unfortunate with the sinful:

> Let the moral sense be awakened and the moral influence
> be established in the minds of the improvident, the unfor-
> tunate, and the depraved. Let them be approached with
> kindness and an ingenuous concern for their welfare. . .[35]

Justice

Of the four principles, the one that has been least subject to perversion is that of justice. What perversion there has been can be found in rigid categorizing rules, the failure, that is, to temper justice with mercy, the sort of rigidity that caused courts of equity to be established in England to temper the law of humankind with the law of God, on the one hand. Or on the other, it may be seen in a modern tendency to equate justice not with equality of opportunity but with equality of success. There can be real debate on how far commutative justice,[36] that which is owing to persons simply by the fact of their existence or being children of God, should go. Does it include, for instance, the right to a minimum income, or to free health care? More particularly, does it include the right to promotion on a job, to tenure in a University, to admission to a course of study, when denial of these benefits has been based on performance rather than on discrimination? Certainly commutative justice needs to be balanced to some degree by distributive justice, or that which is owing to persons in relation to their contribution to society. The problem has been that for most of history commutative justice has had to take very much of a second place to distributive.

Indeed these four principles, in pure or perverted forms, have had periods of popularity and times at which they had little influence. Yet they constitute the basic motives for the care of and help to the poor.

Charity and Judgmentalism

Alms and the Tithe

As we have seen, the idea of equalizing social conditions for love's sake did not last very long. The church, which was both the conscience of the people and the dispenser of the tithe, had to recognize that the poor would not "cease from the land" and would need individual assistance. This clearly had to be done by alms given by the rich and by the distribution of the tithe. The situation was complicated, both by the belief that God must have created the poor for some purpose of his own, and by what might be called a sneaking suspicion that the poor were more moral than the rich. Some passages in the Bible, notably the statement about the camel and the eye of the needle [37] would suggest this, and, as Troeltsch remarks:

> Since the characteristics of the evangelical ethic were self-denial and the severity of its demands it seemed, inversely, as though everything which was difficult, self-denying and contrary to nature were a service to God demanded by the Gospel.[38]

This was further complicated by the Church's belief in an imminent Second Coming, by its unwillingness to become too much involved in the secular world, and by the confusion between those who were poor for religious reasons and those who were simply in need. It becomes, in fact, difficult sometimes to distinguish which group an early writer is discussing, or whether he is referring to both. The tithe was used to support both groups.

The Truly Needy

But immediately the question arose: Were these people really in need? Were not some of them, at least, merely pretending to be poor? And would they spend what was given to them for their support in riotous living or immorality? This is, and was, an important prudential question which bedevils us today. Johnny Cash sings of the "Welfare Cadillac." The tendency is, because there are always a few who abuse any system, to be suspicious of all. The problem is two-fold. Not only are people quick to make moral judgments on others when they have not experienced the temptations to which the other has been subject, and to be particularly hard on sins to which they are themselves most liable – the supposed sins of the poor and those of the rich are often different. But as Basil said in the Fourth Century and is still very obvious today, it takes great experience to distinguish between those who are really poor and those who beg only in order to collect money. [39]

Erring in the Direction of Generosity

The reaction of many of the writers in the church was to stress the importance of helping the poor even at the risk of assisting some who were undeserving.

Clement of Alexandria, at the beginning of the third century, says, "For by being fastidious and setting thyself to try who are fit for thy benevolence, and who are not, it is possible that thou mayest neglect some who are the friends of God."[40] The sense of the poor being in some ways God's special favorites may have influenced him. A century later, Gregory of Nanianzen (or Nanzianus) saw unwise gifts to the undeserving as a lesser evil than overlooking the deserving,[41] a lesson one might hope some people would attend to today. Ambrose counsels the almsgiver to "seek out him who blushes to be discovered."[42]

Chrysostom – Never Be Over-exact

By far the most sweeping assertion was made by Chrysostom, at the end of the Fourth Century. John of Antioch, nicknamed "Chrysostom," or the golden-mouthed and "the apostle of charity," was a lawyer turned churchman who became Patriarch of Constantinople and was banished by the Empress for his criticisms of her behavior. In relation to charity he went back to its original source in the unmerited grace of God. "And yet be we as large hearted as we may," he wrote, "we shall never be able to contribute such love towards man as we stand in need of at the hand of a God that loveth man."[43]

It is, however, the state of the soul of the giver, rather than the need of the recipient, which concerns him most. He continues:

> How then is it other than monstrous, when we are in need of so many things ourselves, to be over-exact with our fellow servants and do all that we can against ourselves? For thou doest not in this way so much prove him unworthy of thy liberality, as thyself of God's love toward men. For he that deals over-exactly with his fellow-servant will be the more sure to find the like treatment at God's hand.[44]

And again:

> When therefore thou art going to God to ask forgiveness
> for thy sins, then call these words to mind, and thou wilt
> know thou deservest to have these things said to thee by
> God, much more than the poor man by thee. And yet God
> hath never said such words to thee as, "Stand off, since thou
> art an impostor, always coming to church, and hearing my
> laws, but when abroad, seeking gold, and pleasure, and
> friendship, and in fact anything above My Commandments.
> And now thou makest thy self humble, but when thy prayers
> are over thou art bold, and cruel, and inhuman. Get thee
> hence, therefore, and never come to Me anymore."[45]

On the basis of this theology Chrysostom was able to assert that "the
poor have only one recommendation: their need. If he be the most perverse of all men, should he lack necessary food, we ought to appease his
hunger,"[46] a sentiment that one can hardly find echoed until the Twentieth Century. He even had empathy for those who asked alms unneces-
sarily, recognizing that the poor might be under a greater temptation
than the rich:

> Dost thou not shudder, man, and blush to call him an im-
> postor for bread? Why even supposing he is practicing im-
> posture he deserves to be pitied for it, because he is so
> pressed with famine as to put on such a character. This then
> is a reproach to our cruelty. For since we have not the heart
> to bestow with readiness, they are compelled to practice a
> great many arts, so as to put a cheat off upon our in-
> humanity, and soften down our harshness.

He does add:

> Now if it was gold and silver he asked of thee, then there
> would be some reason in thy suspicions. But if it is neces-
> sary food that he comes to thee for, why be showing wise
> so unseasonably and take so over-exact an account of him,
> accusing him of idleness or sloth. [47]

14

Chrysostom's answer to the problem of the moral effect of giving on the recipient was essentially that one could not and should not judge.

The problem, however, persisted. As early as the turn of the First Century Ignatius warned against slaves being desirous of freedom purchased through the common fund "lest they be found the slaves of lust."[48]

Good Will

Probably the most sensible answer was that of Ambrose. He believed that the only answer to the problem was the intent of the giver, which he called "good will." It was wrong, he said, to give an extravagant man the means to live extravagantly, or to an adulterer to pay for his adultery, for there would be no good will in it.[49] But one could not be held responsible if one gave in good-will and the recipient then used one's gift wrongly. For this Thomas Aquinas, who followed Ambrose in this belief, was criticized in the Twentieth Century by C. S. Loch, who held that charity that does not have "moral results" cannot be called "moral."[50]

Merit in the Giver

The Good of the Giver

While Loch's criticism of Aquinas shows the reforming trend that had replaced true charity, he is at least concerned with what happens to the recipient of charity and this was what was lacking in some parts of the Christian community throughout the Early and Middle Ages.

Despite Chrysostom's empathy with the supposed impostor, he was much more concerned with the hardness of heart of the giver than with the effects of his charity. And despite his understanding of the unmerited grace of God, Chrysostom was not free of the belief that man, through his own efforts, could win treasure in Heaven. He believed that the poor were "useful" to the rich so that the rich might get rid of their substance and so win that treasure.[51] Other writers were of the same mind. In the apocryphal gospel, *The Shepherd of Hermas*, for instance, the role of the poor is to pray for the soul of the rich.[52]

A Work to Earn Salvation

Gradually love for God's creatures was superseded by self-love, and charity became a "work" through which salvation could be assured. Uhlhorn finds evidence of this as early as Tertullian in the Second Century[53] and in the rejection of Montanism.[54] However, the emphasis given to almsgiving as a "work" may have been due in part to a historical accident. When Christianity became the official religion of the Empire, martyrdom was no longer available as a sure passport to Heaven. The church sought for a substitute. Fasting was already considered such and almsgiving was now added. Uhlhorn quotes Origen and Cyprian to support him.[55] Cyprian certainly summed up this self-fulfilling view of charity, when he characterizes charity as:

> needful for the weak, glorious for the strong, assisted by which the Christian accomplishes spiritual grace, deserves well of Christ the Judge, accounts God his debtor. [56]

So strongly was this believed that Augustine warns against the assumption that one might obtain a license to sin through giving alms. [57]

A Long Silence

This assumption was the major heresy of the medieval church. It may account for the fact that there is virtually no writing, for a millenium or more, until the Fifteenth Century, at least, that is concerned with the plight of the poor or recognizes their problem. The emphasis is almost entirely on the self-fulfillment, in this world or the next, of the giver of alms. Outside of Francis of Assisi, whose love was for all of God's creatures and was accompanied by a vast humility that transcended all economic and social barriers, almost the only writer who appears as the advocate of the poor would seem to be the poet Langland.

Langland — Justice and Joy

Langland's long, rambling fourteenth–century narrative poem is remarkable in a number of ways. Although he has a great sympathy for the poor and his work was used by John Ball and others to fuel enthusiasm for the Peasant's Revolt and by the Wycliffites,[57] he himself believed in the medieval order, which he saw as being corrupted by greed. He rejected the communistic teachings of the Wycliffites. He criticized workmen for making exhorbitant demands for wages: "Save he hath high wages, else will he chide."[59]

At the same time, he demanded justice, rather than simple charity, "which the poor man dare plead / to have allowance of his Lord . of rightful judge he asketh."[60] And, what was much more remarkable, he called for "Some manner joy / Either here or elsewhere . else it were ruth / For amiss he were made . who was not made for joy."[61] This joy, which Langland compares to that of the "wild worms (snakes) in the wood" at the coming of Spring [62] is an entirely new element in consider-

ing the needs of the poor. Langland also restores to charity some of its
original meaning of valuing its recipient. Charity, an allegorical figure:

> . . .rejoices with the joyful . and is generous to the wicked
> Loving and believing . in all that our Lord made. . .
> He tends at other times . to take a pilgrimage
> To ask pardon of the poor . and of those in prison.
> Though he bring them no bread . he bears them sweeter
> life
> Loving them as our Lord had bidden . looking how they
> are.[63]

His description of the poor does, however, stress their patience, a
favorite theme of his:

> Old men and hoar . that be helpless and needy,
> And women with child . that cannot work,
> Blind men and bed ridden . and broken in their members,
> And all poor sufferers . patient under God's sending
> As lepers and mendicants . men fallen into mischief
> Prisoners and pilgrims . and men robbed perchance,
> Or brought low by liars . and their goods lost,
> Or through fire or through flood . fallen to poverty. . .[64]

The Failure of Private Charity

In general, however, private charity failed in its mission, which is perhaps what moved John Knox to write at the end of the Middle Ages:

> Every several Kirk must provide for the poore within the
> self; for fearful and horrible it is, that the poore, quhom
> nott onlie God the Father in his law, but Christ Jesus in his
> evangell, and the Holy Spreit speaking by Sanct Paul, hath
> so earnestlie commended to our cayre, ar universallie so
> contempned and dispysed.[65]

It is also perhaps the reason why Ambrose,[66] and later Aquinas, discussed the care of the poor under the heading of justice rather than that
of charity. The former went as far as to state that "Nature, therefore, has
produced a common right for all, but greed has made it a right for the
few."[67] Aquinas could recognize a "certain moral debt" towards the poor,
but stopped short of creating a legal one.[68] He also came within

measurable distance of calling for a Welfare State. The state, he writes, is concerned with "the provision of those material and external helps the use of which is necessary to virtuous action."[69]

There were probably several reasons why he did not establish a legal right to relief. One was his concern with the higher echelons of law -- Divine Law, Revealed Law, and Natural Law, of which he saw statute or human law as a reflection. He was a philosopher and a theologian, not a lawyer in the modern sense who "makes" law, but one who searches for what law is. Second, he held commutative justice to be less important than distributive justice, and both of them subordinate to general justice which assured concord and order in society.[70] As a modern commentator has it:

> The flower and fruit of justice, therefore, is order and concord in society. It begets a state or condition in society wherein everyone will be able with most probability to perfect his nature and develop his personality, thus tending to his ultimate end, union with God.[71]

It is probable that legal rights for the poor would not conduce to this harmony, at least in such a believer in hierarchy as Aquinas, although he, too, sees beyond a mere government subsidy to a debt owed to everyone.

Finally, perhaps, Aquinas' emphasis on the virtue of Prudence affected his thinking. Prudence is generally listed as the first of the Cardinal Virtues, the other three being temperance, fortitude, and justice, although not the source of the others, as pride is of the deadly sins. Prudence has to do with what is wise or politic: one dictionary defines it as "control of conduct in the light of consequences." It is perhaps significant that in the major attempt to reconcile Aquinas' teaching with modern social work practice, his major contribution is seen to be his concept of prudence and it is held that "it is only insofar as we are superior to others that we can be of help to them, supplying their needs."[72]

The Church and the Marginal People

Yet, in one respect at least, the medieval church was the protector of the poor. Only the church was big enough and universal enough to speak for those who were outside the system. The Feudal system, through its reciprocal responsibilities, could be counted on to take care of most people, even the poor, in some way or other. But it was not structured to take care of the sick, the migrant, or the fugitive. It is perhaps sig-

18

nificant that the three services most typical of the church at that time were the hospital, the hospice, and sanctuary. The church could also act as the conscience of mankind towards the outcast and the unpopular. With the fragmentation of the church this bulwark was lost and did not appear, in America, until the Federal Government assumed something of this role in the 1930s.

Individualizing the Poor

Civic Responsibility

In the first half of the Sixteenth Century, and perhaps only in two cities of the Spanish colony of the Netherlands (there is, as far as I am aware, no record of the system being tried elsewhere), a model for a new relationship between the rich and the poor was adumbrated. Juan Luis Vives' plans for the support of the poor in the cities of Bruges [73] and Ypres [74] are seen by de Schweinitz as steps towards social security largely because they were civic rather than church-administered plans. They made use of what he called the prototype of the modern social worker, and they employed the device of more or less individualized investigation. This last was certainly something new, and something that was to be virtually lost in Protestant Europe in the very near future. The plans, although they were to be administered by the city rather than the church, were submitted to the theological faculty at the Sorbonne, which found them to be in agreement with the scriptures, the teaching of the Apostles, and the laws of the Church, "hard but wholesome."[75] There is, however, no mention of the Deity in them, and it is Nature, rather than God, who has put rich and poor together.

View of the Poor

The plans are not without some moralism. There is still the problem of the "undeserving poor." "Those who have dissipated their fortunes in riotous living," for instance, are to be assigned the most irksome tasks: "they must not die of hunger, but they must feel its pangs." Severity should be shown to "strong and lusty beggars who have no lust to work" and although there should be an inquiry into the morals of the poor, this should be extended also to the children of the rich.[76]

But the poor are not seen as a class. There is no suggestion that they are, as a whole, sinful or that they exist merely to provide the means of salvation for the rich. Indeed the exact opposite is true. "For no other cause did nature mingle poor and rich together but that poor men should receive benefits of rich men."[77] The poor had become important in their own right and as individuals.

There is no passion to reform them. The prefects are enjoined to get knowledge of their condition, their health, but also "their secret and homely griefs" and, if possible, their merits.[78] Work is to be found for them, not in general because they are thought to be workshy, but because they need work. Some of the blind are to be encouraged to study, "for in them we see an aptitude for learning by no means to be despised."[79] Other blind persons have an aptitude for music, having sharpened one sense due to the loss of another. The theme throughout is personal interest in people who are without means of support but who are in many ways one's equals.

They are to be visited not only by the appointed prefects, but by the families of the well-to-do, and, if food be brought it should be in the form of specially prepared dishes and not just left-overs from the tables of the rich:

> so that the citizen's children may learn to visit and love the poor men's little cottages and the good man of the house and the good wife may remember that the burden of their neighbor's calamities must be relieved not only with alms but also with their presence in visiting, comforting, helping, and executing the deeds of pity. . .[80]

This is new indeed. It is humanism at its best. It might not have been practicable except in a community of fairly stable burghers and peasants, but Vives, it should be remembered, was the representative of a colonial power, besides being a scholar who in his time was considered the equal and even the superior of Erasmus, and had been tutor to the future Queen of England.

Catholic Humanism

This was probably the finest flower of Catholic humanism, conjoining charity and responsibility and with an interest in this world as well as perhaps in the next. DeSchweinitz draws the line from Vives, through Vincent de Paul, with his amazing insight that if we served the poor long enough, they might learn to forgive us,[81] to the "Christian Socialists" of the later Nineteenth Century. However, Vives had none of the reforming tendencies of the latter. He is closer, to my mind, to Thomas Chalmers, not so much in his use of investigation of an individual's needs, but in the status he accords to the poor. He is also in the line that ended with the social Encyclicals, and perhaps with Pius XI's warning that although justice might come first and "charity cannot take the place of justice unfairly withheld. . . in its [Charity's] absence the wisest regulations come to nothing." Pius looks to a time when:

> the rich and others in power will change their former negligence of their poorer brethren with solicitous and effective regard; will listen with kindly feeling to their just complaints, and will readily forgive them the faults and mistakes they possibly make.[82]

It is interesting to see however, how much both Pius and Leo XIII before him[83] rely on the Angelic doctor, Aquinas, and his commutative justice.

The Poor and the Social Order

Social Upheaval and Public Policy

In the period between the virtual end of the Feudal system and the full establishment of the Protestant ethic, most nations developed systems of public relief. It was a period of great hardship for the poor. Sir Thomas More, perhaps the first after Langland to speak in defense of the poor, was critical of the rich, who, he thought, should be restrained by law and not permitted to "bie up al, to ingrosse, and forestalle, and with their monopolie to keepe the market alone as please them."[84] He was also opposed to the death penalty for theft – a man many centuries ahead of his time. Of the poor, dispossessed by enclosures, he writes:

> By one meanes therfor or by other, either by hook or croke they muste needes departe awaye, pore, selyve, wretched soules, men, women, husbands, wives, fatherless children, widowes, wofull mothers, with their yonge babes, and their whole houshold smal in substance. . .Awaye they trudge, I say, out of their knowen and accustomed houses, fyndynge no place to rest in. All there housholdestuffe, whiche is verye litle woorthe,. . .they be constrayned to sell it for a thing of naught. And when they have wandered abrode tyll that be spent, what can they then else doo but steale, and then justly pardy be hanged, or els go about beggyng. And yet then also they be caste in prison as vagaboundes, because they go aboute and worke not: whome no man will

21

set at worke, though they never so willyngly profre themselves therto.[85]

Regulating the Poor

The last sentence is significant, for the measures that set up public
relief were always accompanied by stricter and stricter laws against begging and indeed leaving one's settlement, never mind if one had been
dispossessed. On could be branded, enslaved, or even executed (on a
third offense) for begging. Sydney and Beatrice Webb are of the opinion
that public relief sprang from no motive of compassion for the poor; it
was a measure introduced to avert public disorder:

> . . .the King, his Council and his Parliament were enacting
> and carrying out laws. . .of a character exactly opposite to
> that of the almsgiving of the mediaeval church or that of
> the benevolent institutions established by pious founders,
> Craft Guilds and municipal corporations. All these ac-
> tivities were derived from the obligation of the Christian to
> relieve the suffering of "God's poor." The King and his
> nobles were intent upon an altogether different object,
> namely maintaining order. . .[86]

They do, however, speak of a "new statecraft relative to destitution"
and suggest that neither repression nor what they describe as "fortuitous
distribution of voluntary gifts to necessarily selected individuals" was prov-
ing adequate to the task and:

> ubiquitous provision had to be made locally by some organ
> of government for all those who were actually in need of
> the means of existence, whatever the cause of their destitu-
> tion. . .[87]

Piven and Cloward, writing at the end of the turbulent 1960s and tend-
ing to see all welfare measures as attempts to control the poor, suggest
that Henry VIII and his counselors were actually intent on destroying
the system of charity that had existed up to that time, and see this, by
inference, as one of the reasons for the dissolution of the monasteries.[88]
The Webbs were convinced that Henry's actions were actuated entirely
by a selfish desire to retain the privileges of the rich.[89]

The Role of Order
They may have been, but one should not forget what order meant to
the Sixteenth Century. It was ordained by God and any threat to it was
a blasphemy. That the old order was crumbling must have seemed like
the beginning of unimaginable chaos.[90] Bismarck was accused of much
the same motive in introducing the first social insurance in the 1880s. It
was hard to believe that the Iron Chancellor had any compassion for the
poor, but G. M. Trevelyan says of the Privy Council in James I and II's
time that, "it had a real regard for the interests of the poor, with which
the interests of public order were much involved."[91] A desire for order
is not necessarily totally self-seeking.

Overseers
As a matter of fact both church-sponsored charity and public relief
seem to have co-existed for some time. In many communities it was sixty
or seventy years before the "poor-sess" was even collected or an Overseer of the poor appointed. Private donors gave their money to the
churchwardens who carried out a number of welfare operations, including direct payments both to parishioners and to itinerant beggars who
were licensed as having been victims of a calamity, such as a fire or im-
prisonment or the death of their husbands at sea, the "boarding out" and
later apprenticeship of orphan children, the burial of strangers who died
in the parish, the relief of other communities which had experienced fires
or epidemics, including in the case of a small English village, the city of
"Montreal in America," and the maintenance of almshouses (not institutions, but cottages for the elderly).[92] Most of these duties seem to have
been carried out with considerable compassion, but the amounts given
depended on whether there was money in the "poor-box."

Residence
One of the most important duties of the overseers, however, and the
churchwardens before them, especially after the Settlement Act of 1662,
was removing "strangers" from the parish, and even preventing them from
entering it.[93] Bona fide travelers were helped, but not those looking for
work or for alms. This insistence on helping only those who were born
or had lived a long time in the parish was a new concept, instituted to
try to control a population that was necessarily on the move as agricultural land was put out to pasture and feudal bonds were dissolved. It
persisted in America, and is still the occasion for jurisdictional disputes
today, although residence requirements for relief were declared unconstitutional in 1969. Some will remember the attempts on the part of the

State of California to prevent refugees from the Dust Bowl entering California in the 1930s and the number of children shipped back from that State to places where they had, at best, tenuous legal residence. This is a far cry from Chryostom's appeal to the citizens of Alexandria to relieve those who came to the city because they were attracted by its generosity,[94] perhaps remembering Matthew 5:47, "And if you salute only your brethren, what more are you doing than others? Do not even the Gentiles do the same?"

Chrysostom was probably not confronted by the same social conditions as were the well-to-do in England from the Sixteenth to the Eighteenth Centuries. Some writers hold that only the relief system kept the poor from open revolt, such as had occurred two centuries before under John Ball and Wat Tyler, and that in this way insurrection was prevented through the Nineteenth Century despite occasional outbursts of Chartism and Luddism.[95]

A Moral Evaluation

But it needed more than a fear of disorder to arrive at a point where people were willing to "leave the poor and the needy to the punishment which a righteous God has inflicted on them."[96] It needed a moral evaluation, as it is expressed in the title of two well-known tracts of the Seventeenth and early Eighteenth Centuries: *Stanley's Remedy, or the Way to Reform Wandering Beggars, Thieves, Highway Robbers and Pickpockets: or an Abstract of his Discovery, Wherein it is Shown that Sodom's Sin of Idleness is the Poverty and Misery of This Kingdom* or the author of *Robinson Crusoe's Giving Alms no Charity and Employing the Poor a Grievance to the Nation*.[97] It needed, in fact, the Reformation and the subsequent perversion of the Reformed theology.

24

Notes

The Problem

[1] Deuteronomy 5:11.

[2] *De Officio Ministrorum*, I, xxxii.

[3] *Seventeenth Homily on Second Corinthians*.

[4] See Max Weber, The Protestant Ethic and the Spirit of Capitalism, trans. by Talcott Parson, London, 1930, p. 122.

[5] From a report signed by him, dated 1696 and quoted by Sir Frederick Eden, *The State of the Poor; Or, An History of the Labouring Classes, from the Conquest to the Present Period*, London, 1797, Vol I, p. 38.

[6] He is quoted in an interview with *Newsweek* as saying that material wealth "is God's way of blessing people who put him first." This is reported by James H. Smylie, "Gilder, Gilt and the Needle's Eye," *Presbyterian Outlook*, 164, January 25, 1982: 6.

[7] Thomas Walker, *The Original*, excerpted by Gertrude Lubbuck, *Some Poor Law Questions*, London, 1895, p. 166.

[8] Quoted by Weber, *The Protestant Ethic*, p. 177.

[9] W. Bury, *"Poor Law Progress and Reform,"* Poor Law Conference Reports, London, 1889, p. 319, excerpted by Lubbock, *Some Poor Law Questions*, p. 47.

[10] *Eighth Annual Report of the Board of the State Commission of Public Charities of the State of Illinois*, 1884, excerpted by Sophonisba Breckenridge, ed. *Public Welfare Administration in the United States: Select Documents*, Chicago, 1927, p. 641.

[11] N. Masterman, ed., *Chalmers on Charity: A Selection of Passages and Scenes to Illustrate the Social Teaching and Practical Work of Thomas Chalmers, D.D., Westminster*, 1900, p. 126.

[12] Senator Paul Douglas, in his *Social Security in the United States*, New York, 1936, says that the program is one to permit mothers to bring up their children in their own homes (p. 185) and the President's Committee on Economic Security uses the word "rear" in its Report, p. 36. Margaret Rich, in an article in Russell H. Kurtz, ed., *The Public Assistance Worker*, New York, 1938, pp. 130-44, distinguishes this program from those for the aged and the blind by its "long-time" aspects. The assertion that the program had, even in its "legislative intent" a rehabilitative and short-time purpose is nowadays so common that it needs no documentation. It began about ten years after the Act was passed. In 1937 the Social Security Board made clear that it feared that if a mother were

both homemaker and wage earner, the home would be broken up after she had failed in her dual capacity (*Social Security Board, Social Security in America*, Washington, 1937, pp. 223-224) but by 1942 a social worker advocates a diagnostic approach to the problem with the decision apparently that of the agency's (Frieda Riggs, "Individualizing Employment Planning in Aid to Dependent Children Families," *The Family*, 23, (1942): 297-300) and today the work requirement, even where not spelled out in law, is virtually universal.

[13] Micah 6:8.

[14] Lionel Trilling, *The Liberal Imagination*, New York, 1950, p. 222.

[15] I owe this quotation to Herbert Butterfield's *Christianity and History*, Scribner's Library edition, New York, 1949, pp. 65-66.

The Impulse to Help

[16] Exodus 23:11.

[17] Proverbs 29:7.

[18] According to A. F. Young and E. T. Ashton, *British Social Work in the Nineteenth Century*, New York, 1956, pp. 82-84. It is a recognized weakness of this book that I have not examined in detail the development of Jewish thought. The Jews have made a contribution to helping the poor out of proportion to their numbers through their insistence on justice, their sense of community, their unwillingness to consider a poor person undeserving until this was proved, and their insistence that relief be adequate. But these have been largely correctives to the prevailing Christian practice and somewhat confined to the Jewish Community. The best account I know of the basic principles of Jewish treatment of the unfortunate is in Herbert Aptekar's *The Dynamics of Casework and Counselling*, Boston, 1955. Also of some interest is Alfred J. Kutzik's *Social Work and Jewish Values*, Washington, 1959.

[19] Romans 3:23.

[20] G. Uhlhorn, *Christian Charity in the Ancient Church,* Edinburgh, 1883, p. 38.

[21] Leon Lallemand, *Histoire de la Charité,* Paris, 1902-6, Vol 1, p. 139.

[22] Karl de Schweinitz, *England's Road to Social Security*, Philadelphia, 1943, p. 22.

[23] "All Things Bright and Beautiful," by Cecil Frances Alexander, 1845. The verse was still printed in *Hymns Ancient and Modern*, 1924 edition.

[24] An excellent source of understanding the "chain of being" is E. M. W. Tillyard's *The Elizabethan World View*, London, 1945 and a brilliant

analysis of the problem of order in *Macbeth*, L. C. Knight's *How Many Children Had Lady Macbeth?*, Cambridge, 1931.

[25] For a discussion of the difference between empathy, sympathy, and pity the reader is referred to the author's *Giving and Taking Help*, Chapel Hill, 1972, pp. 79-80.

[26] Edmund Gibson, Bishop of Lincoln, *The Peculiar Excellency and Reward of Supporting Schools of Charity*, quoted by Betsy Rogers, *The Cloak of Charity*, London, 1949, p. 11.

[27] John Wesley, quoted by H. Richard Niebuhr, *The Social Sources of Denominationalism*, New York, 1929: Living Age edition, pp. 70-71.

[28] Sir Thomas Browne, *Religio Medici*, quoted by de Schweinitz, *England's Road*, p. 14.

[29] Ernest Troeltsch, *The Social Teaching of the Christian Churches*, trans. by Olive Wyon, New York, 1931, Vol. I, p. 37.

[30] 2 Thessalonians 3:10, "If anyone will not work, let him not eat."

[31] *The Constitution of the Apostles*, 4:3.

[32] Much of the energy of welfare workers in this country is expended in seeing that no one who does not "deserve" (is eligible for) public assistance gets it, although the excessive individualization of the program actually makes cheating easier. The British, in establishing their Health Services, were aware that some foreigners would take advantage of it, but decided that a system of checks on eligibility would be both cost-ineffective and degrading.

[33] 2 Thessalonians 3:6-12.

[34] Matthew 7:1, Luke 6:37, Romans 2:1 ff.

[35] *Annual Report of the Society for the Prevention of Pauperism*, quoted by Edward Devine, *The Principles of Relief*, New York, 1904, p. 292.

[36] The term is Thomas Aquinas'. See *Summa Theologica*, II-II, Q.117.

Charity and Judgmentalism

[37] This appears in all three Synoptic gospels, at Matthew 19:24, Mark 10:25, and Luke 18:25.

[38] Troeltsch, *The Social Teaching*, p. 103.

[39] Quoted by Uhlhorn, *Christian Charity*, p. 269.

[40] *Quis Divas Salvatur,* xiii.

[41] Quoted by Uhlhorn, *Christian Charity*, pp. 269-270.

[42] *De Officio,* II, xvi.

[43] *Fourteenth Homily on the Book of Romans.*

[44] Ibid.

[45] Ibid.

46 *Fourth Homily on Lazarus.*
47 *Fourteenth Homily on the Book of Romans.*
48 *Epistle to Polycarp*, iv.
49 *De Officio*, I, xxx.
50 C. S. Loch, *Charity and Social Life*, London, 1910, p. 260-261.

Merit in the Giver

51 *Seventeenth Homily on Second Corinthians.*
52 *The Shepherd of Hermas*, III, iii, "The Similitude of the Elm and the Vine."
53 Uhlhorn, *Charity in the Ancient Church*, p. 150.
54 Ibid., pp. 206-211.
55 Ibid., p. 213.
56 Quoted, in this instance, by Lillian Brandt, *How Much Shall I Give?* New York, 1921, p. 85.
57 *De Civitate Dei*, XXI, articles 21 and 27.
58 See Christopher Dawson, *Mediaeval Religion and Other Essays*, London, 1934, pp. 181-184. The following quotations are taken from Dawson's translation. A fuller rendering of some of these passages is given by Nevill Coghill, *Visions From Piers Plowman*, London, 1949, but I prefer Dawson's text as closer to the original. The actual title of the poem is *The Vision of William about Piers the Plowman and Visions of the Same about Do-Well, Do-Better and Do-Best*. There are three versions, usually referred to as A, B, and C and dating from the 1360s to the 1390s.
59 *Piers The Plowman*, A, vii, 300.
60 Ibid., C, xvi, 289-291.
61 Ibid., C, xvi, 299-301.
62 Ibid., C, xvi, 293-297.
63 Coghill translation, reference not given, but probably B, xv.
64 *Piers The Plowman*, C, x, 175-182.
65 John Knox, *Buke of Discipline*, 1560. Actually Knox was chairman of the committee which compiled it. It was edited and reproduced by David Laing in Volume II of his six volume *Works of John Knox*, Edinburgh, 1846-1864. The passage quoted is on p. 200.
66 *De Officio*, I, xxxii.
67 Ibid., I, xxviii.
68 *Summa Theologica* II-II, Q.117.
69 *De Regemine Principium*, I, i5.
70 *Summa Theologica*, II-II, Q.63.

28

[71] George V. Dougherty, "The Moral Basis of Social Order According to S. Thomas," *Philosophical Studies of the Catholic University of America*, 63 (1941): 53.

[72] Mary J. McCormick, *Diagnostic Casework in the Thomistic Pattern*, New York, 1954, especially p. 196. There is also a Thomistic "school" of social work today, whose chief characteristic is the use of reason. See Herbert H. Stroup, "The Minister and the Thomistic Social Worker," *Iliff Review*, 67, 2 (Spring 1960): 53.

[73] *De Subventione Pauperum*, 1531. This has been translated by Margaret M. Sherwood and is excerpted in de Schweinitz, *England's Road to Social Security*, p. 32

Individualizing the Poor

[74] *Forma subventionis Pauperum*, 1535, translated by William Marshall, and also excerpted by de Schweinitz, *England's Road*, p. 34.

[75] De Schweinitz, *England's Road*, p. 36.

[76] *De Subventionis*, excerpted by de Schweinitz, p. 32.

[77] *Forma Subventionis*, excerpted by de Schweinitz, p. 35.

[78] Ibid., p. 34.

[79] *De Subventionis*, p. 32.

[80] *Forma Subventionis*, p. 35.

[81] Despite the researches of a number of Catholic friends, I have been unable to locate this statement.

[82] *Quadragessimo Anno*, 1930, reproduced in Anton C. Pegis, *The Wisdom of Catholicism*, New York, 1947, p. 762.

[83] *Rerum Novarum*, 1891.

The Poor and The Social Order

[84] Sir Thomas More, *Utopia*, Everyman Edition, p. 21.

[85] Ibid., p. 20.

[86] Sidney and Beatrice Webb, *English Poor Law History*, Part. I, p. 29, quoted from Frances Fox Piven and Richard A. Cloward, *Regulating the Poor*, New York, 1971, p. 15.

[87] Ibid., p. 23 (B. & S. Webb); p. 12 (Piven and Cloward).

[88] Piven and Cloward, *Regulating the Poor*, p. 15.

[89] Sydney and Beatrice Webb, *English Poor Law History*, Part I, p. 25 reproduced by Piven and Cloward, p. 15.

[90] See earlier discussion of the Chain of Being, especially note 24.

[91] G. M. Trevelyan, *English Social History: A Survey of Six Centuries: Chaucer to Queen Victoria*, London, quoted from Webb and Webb, *English Poor Law History*, pp.170-171, by Piven and Cloward, *Regulating the Poor*, p. 16.

[92] These examples are all taken from G. E. Hubbard, *The Old Book of Wye,* Derby, 1951, which is a study of the churchwarden's accounts in an English parish from the time of Henry VIII to that of Charles II. These examples and many others are found on pp. 110-136.

[93] Hubbard reports a churchwarden's expense for a journey "to prevent Dunkes coming to the parish," *The Old Book of Wye*, p. 114.

[94] *Fourteenth Homily on Romans*.

[95] Piven and Cloward quote J. S. Mill and G. N. Trevelyan in support of this contention, *Regulating the Poor*, p. 20.

[96] Reinhold Niebuhr, *The Contribution of Religion to Social Work*, New York, 1932, p. 16.

[97] Dated 1646 and 1704 respectively.

CHAPTER 2

Toward Judgmentalism and Individualism: The Reformation to the Nineteenth Century

The Work Ethic and Election

Contempt Not Intrinsic to Reformed Theology

There is nothing in Reformed theology that in itself should have led to such a contempt for the poor, such a lumping together of the victim of misfortune, the supposedly depraved and the improvident, such a desire to reform them or make life miserable for them so that they would reform themselves. This now became the rule and dominated the relationship between rich and poor for two centuries or more. We have seen John Knox's "horror" at the way he saw the poor as being treated.[1] Calvin was as suspicious of riches as was Wesley later. A theology in which works, as opposed to faith, were totally ineffectual might have dried up the beneficence of the rich, but it should not have led to the utter contempt for the poor. All men were sinners; there was now "no distinction;" there was nothing a man could do to earn favor with God. The granting of Grace is His prerogative and His alone. Some He chooses, others He denies, not according to any canon of human justice, but for purposes of His own. This would look to be a breeding ground for humility and not for sweeping judgments on one's fellows.

Yet it proved to be exactly the opposite. Not only were the poor despised – the thing that had so horrified Knox – but they were treated as if each one of them had the characteristics of the least worthy. This was not a personal judgment, based on knowledge of a person's individual circumstances. Mill, in his *Political Economy*, ascribed this to the necessity for a rule of law, rather than men. The state, he writes, "cannot undertake to discriminate between the deserving and the undeserving indigent,"[2] but this does not account for the judgment made on the poor as a class.

The Role of Work

There have been a number of explanations, theological and economic, for what happened.[3] One of these is Luther's emphasis on work as a necessity. Work, in the thinking of the medieval church, was a divinely ordained means of existence, a means to asceticism, of fulfilling the Natural Order and insuring justice. Work was educative, serving the ends of punishment and discipline, a *remedium peccati*,[4] but it was not necessary to salvation, or something owed by the worker to God. There was none of Luther's "evaluation of the fulfillment of duty in worldly affairs as the highest form which the moral activity of the individual could assume."[5]

Yet, Luther did not have in mind the necessity to engage in a gainful occupation at whatever wages were offered. He was arguing that a workman was fulfilling God's intention as well, or better, than the hermit or the man given to the contemplative life. He equates giving to monasteries, cloisters, churches, chapels and, in particular, mendicant friars with giving to "vagabonds and desperate rogues."[6] But it took the needs of the new capitalist economy for dutiful workers to translate this involvement in worldly affairs into a demand that man's first duty was to earn his own living, even after, as a writer nearly fifty years ago put it, "the necessity of work, for whatever end and of whatever kind, is no longer a self-evident truth."[7]

Those among the poor who either could not find work or were too sick to work were the natural victims of this demand. It has always been an inconsistent one. The demand has never been made of those who have inherited money. Cotton Mather did, it is true, consider loss of time through sleep a wickedness, but chiefly as time lost from the service of God rather than as a failure to earn his own living.

Other writers ascribe the particular application of the work ethic in America, where it has certainly persisted longer and more forcefully than anywhere else, to the demands of a frontier economy and the fact that any reasonably competent person could scratch a living out of the wilderness. Consequently, those who could not or did not were naturally seen as inferior. It is, however, interesting to note that in the supposedly ruggedly individualistic colonial days, relief was still necessary. A study in 1949 showed that the relief rate in Virginia was actually higher in 1759 than it was nearly two hundred years later.[8]

Assurance of Election

But the new evaluation of work was not the sole factor operating. Weber and Tawney believe that the crux of the matter was to be found in the doctrine of election and the "absolute duty" of the elect to "consider himself chosen, and to combat all doubts as temptations of the devil, since lack of self-confidence is the result of insufficient faith and hence of imperfect faith."[9] This, with the emphasis on worldly activity, meant that one could only be sure that one was one of the elect if one was actively engaged in doing work and that as a corollary, those who

32

did not or could not work showed that they were not of the elect.[10] This led to a hatred of those who did not or could not work as being an insult to God.[11]

But to look for evidences of election in human behavior was to deny the whole rationale of Calvin's doctrine. It meant that God chose those who pleased Him through their activities, and led to the identification of worldly success with election. It opened the door to the possibility that it was man and not God who determined his election. There is a very fine line between a belief that God has chosen those who are successful in life and the proposition that if one can manage to be successful, God will choose one. And this is a wholesale theological reversal. The transcendent God whose ways are not our ways, nor his thoughts our thoughts, has become the embodiment of very human virtues.

Theological Reversal

This theological reversal has been noted by, among others, R. B. Perry and Richard Niebuhr. Perry comments that "if a man believes that God's grace is governed by no principle, or that its principle is wholly inscrutable, he can seek to please God only by the degree of his humility."[12] This, he adds, was inconsistent with the self-reliant character of the New England colonist and led to the various Covenant and federal theologies.

Niebuhr emphasizes the personal nature of the religion of the middle classes. Just as success in this world seemed to follow personal worth, so it must be with God. Man could not accept a universe of suprahuman forces in the face of which he was powerless. The only force he could rely on was his own effort. Fortune and misfortune were discounted; so was God's unaccountable Grace.[13] Sin became "not so much a state of mind as a deed or a characteristic; it is not so much the evil with which the whole social life and structure is infected as it is the personal failure of the individual."[14] Tawney remarks that, "Convinced that character is all and circumstance nothing, he sees in the poverty of those who fall by the way, not a misfortune to be pitied and relieved, but a moral failing to be condemned. . ."[15]

To this Perry adds an interesting suggestion: that the Puritan made a moral diagnosis of poverty because morals were within "his sphere of competence: and economics and psychology were not."[16] Given man's tendency to judge his fellows, he will do so in the frame of reference with which he is familiar. Examples of this may be found in many psychologists and social workers today.

Equation of Grace with Wordly Success

But a much more serious heresy arose at this time, one that affected not only the poor but the whole fabric of life and the persistence of which today is a far greater threat to the Gospel than any amount of humanism or secularism. The equation of Grace with wordly success is a heresy, despite the statement attributed to Mr. Falwell, that material wealth is God's way of blessing those who put him first.[17] The covenants made by churches are somewhat presumptuous. They do sound a bit as if God was in some way the equal of the covenanters. That this may be a problem is recognized in the opening sentences of the covenant made by the Northampton, Massachusetts, church:

> Disclaiming any confidence of, or any worthiness in, ourselves to be in covenant with God, or to partake of the least of His mercies, and also all strength of our own to help covenant with Him. . .[18]

There is some recognition, however, of what Paul makes so clear, that morality is a response to the love of God and not a means of earning that love, that Christ died for sinners, that we keep God's law out of gratitude to Him and not to achieve our own salvation. Christ can be held, in fact, to have brought into the world an entirely new relationship between love and morality. The Christian statement is not, "Behave and you will be loved" (if that were so, everyone would be condemned) but, "You are loved; therefore behave."

God's Lieutenants and Case-Aides

But the Puritan did not appear to have recognized this. He may have approached the Cross as a penitent, or, in social work terms, as a most needy client, but he left it as God's lieutenant to enforce the moral law, or, in social work terms again, as His case-aide or probation officer. We can see the beginning of a move in this direction in the writings of C. S. Loch. The significant of the Reformation for charity was, in his opinion, "that the religious life was to be democratic. . .and in a new sense – it was to be moral."[19] Weber also notes the reaction against the medieval church which was "given to punishing the heretic but indulgent to the sinner"[20] and Troeltsch that while Catholicism had distributed the ethical claim unequally among various classes of people, Protestantism demands the same moral standard from all alike.[21] The non-elect poor were the easiest target for those who believed themselves charged with the responsibility of enforcing morality on others.

There is an inconsistency here, to which Calvin himself may have been subject. On the one hand good works and obedience to the Law are responses to God's love. Calvin understood that clearly, "the fruits and evidence of a lively faith" as the Westminster Confession puts it,[22] are performed by the faithful "not at all of themselves, but wholly from the Spirit of Christ"[23] and are totally ineffectual in the matter of salvation.[24] On the other hand the Law is held to be essential to the non-elect, despite the fact that they are damned and can do nothing to escape damnation (their good works cannot please God),[25] "to awaken their conscience to flee from the wrath to come, to drive them to Christ. . . or to leave them inexcusable."[26] This would seem to make it possible for man to reverse God's judgment. While there might be civil reasons for controlling the unregenerate, it is hard to see a religious one.

Modern Gnostics

In trying to understand what had happened, the theories of Erich Voegelin may be of help. Voegelin describes a process that occurs whenever persons attempt to explain matters through their own value systems – that is, without conceding the unknowableness of God. He sees people who create answers to the human predicament and try to order society in accordance with them as "the modern Gnostics," those who believe that they know.

While many of his modern Gnostics operate in a secular, humanistic world – he instances Dewey, Marx, and Freud – he includes Calvin. He is, however, perhaps too ready to ascribe the Gnosticism to the founder of a system, rather than to the founder's disciples, who religiously follow the book and made no accommodation to changing circumstances; the need for a literally inspired dogma is a common human trait. It avoids the need to think. The Gnostic, he says, overcomes the uncertainty of faith by receding from transcendence and endowing man and his intramundane range of action with the meaning of eschatological fulfillment.[27]

He says of the "Saint" that he is "A Gnostic who will not leave the transfiguration of the world to the Grace of God beyond history, but will do the work of God himself, right here and now, in history."[28] The medieval church would probably have called it simply the exercise of superbia, or Pride, the forgetting that one is a creature, and not God.

Depravity

Part of the problem seems to be that the Puritans had the lowest possible estimate of the nature of man. They believed that if man is not controlled by the Law he will inevitably lie, cheat, and prefer to be cared for by others than put out effort on his own. In his natural state he is utterly depraved. Young and Ashton, writing of British social work in the Nineteenth Century, say that the only religious groups, outside of the Jews, who showed some compassion for the poor were the Quakers and the Unitarians, the first because of their belief in the purely immanent Inner Light, and the latter because they were not "hampered by a belief in the depravity of man and original sin."[29]

But the doctrine of Original Sin can and ought to be a corrective to Pride in oneself. What capitalist-puritanism did, and does, is to ascribe Original Sin to others, while denying it, or being convinced that Grace has overcome it, in oneself.

Harshness Rather than Kindness

The most serious consequence, however, of seeing morality as an antecedent to love rather than its fruit is that there is no reason for the insister on morality to be loving towards those whom he attempts to reform. The methods used to try to reform the poor and spur them to independence were nearly all negative. Kindness towards them was suspect. It would tempt them to be content with their state. Josiah Quincy in the early Nineteenth Century criticizes the overseers of the poor:

> In executing the trust they will almost unavoidably be guided by sentiments of pity and compassion, and be very little influenced by consideration of the effect of the facility or fullness of provision to encourage habits of idleness, dissipation and extravagance among the class which labor. They first give necessaries, then comforts; and often, in the end, pamper rather than relieve.[30]

The belief that what will stop people being poor is to make them miserable is one that persists in our society. George Gilder, believed by some to have provided the theological justification for the Reagan administration's economics, is quoted as saying that for the poor to succeed and cease to be poor, they "need most of all the spur of their poverty."[31] He also holds that the "crucial goal should be to restrict the [welfare] system as much as possible, by making it unattractive and even a bit demeaning."[32] He is a true Eighteenth Century man. Indeed, from the Seventeenth to the Nineteenth Centuries there seems to be only one man who appeared to believe the opposite. This was Doctor Samuel

Johnson, a man very conscious of Original Sin in himself, as his letters and diaries show, who wrote:

> Life is a pill which none of us can bear to swallow without gilding; yet for the poor we delight in stuffing it still barer; and are not ashamed to show even visible displeasure if ever the bitter taste is taken from their mouths.[33]

Johnson's surprising remedy was to provide the poor with the means to purchase gin and drown their sorrows.[34]

The concept that one might be more ambitious, more able to risk oneself in the market if one were healthy, well-fed, and felt that one was valued by others appears to have lain dormant from early Christian times to comparatively recent years, with the possible exception of Vives, and as we shall see, Chalmers. Yet it has been shown that, in general, positive reinforcement is a more effective way of changing behavior than is negative.[35] This is, of course, dependent on whether the aim is to change or control behavior, rather than to help the other person to lead a normally satisfying life in which he can develop his own personality.

Spurring the Poor to Independence

The Workhouse

There are in general four ways in which society has tried to spur the poor to independence or to correct their morals.

The first is simply to make the life of the pauper as uncomfortable as one can. This was the thinking behind the Workhouse Test. In order to receive relief, one had to be willing to enter the Workhouse, which, in Young and Ashton's words, meant that relief in the workhouse was made as uncomfortable as possible by irksome regulations, few social amenities, poor food and a general and deliberate encouragement of gloom and despondency.[36]

Thomas Chalmers, who opposed the Workhouse test, said about it at the beginning of the Nineteenth Century, "Their paupers are met by the same treatment as their criminals."[37] Trevelyan calls Workhouses "penal settlements for the unfortunate" but adds that the proliferation of them after the Poor Law Reform of 1834 drew attention to their shortcomings, and led to such exposés as *Oliver Twist*. Dickens, he said, "appealed from the Benthamite abstractions in which the Commissioners dealt, to the flesh and blood realities which interested the more sensitive rising generation of the new Victorian era."[38] De Schweinitz reports that only seven percent of infants born in or received into workhouses survived for two years.[39]

Less-Eligibility

The second method employed was that of less-eligibility, and is perhaps best illustrated by the statement of Baron Kaspar von Voght in the 1790's. Although six-sevenths of the poor were women and children and were not receiving cash relief but were being put to work at spinning flax in their own homes, "it was our determined principle to reduce this support lower than what any industrious man or woman could earn."[40] Other definitions were even stricter: the standard of relief must be lower than could be earned by "an independent laborer of the lowest class,"[41] for instance. When a person was incapable of working, even through no fault of his or her own, he or she must receive less than the lowest-paid worker. Other societies have not been so niggardly. The Danish welfare system, for instance, has a long-standing aversion to less-eligibility and a "fundamental precept that the pension. . . should be sufficient for the requirements of the pensioner and his family."[42]

Diminished Legal Status

The third method is pauperism, or according a diminished legal status to the pauper. Edith Abbott, writing in 1940, says that at that time there were fourteen states in the United States which denied paupers the right to vote, four by constitutional provision.[43] She quotes a case in which a State Supreme Court upheld the right of a Poor Law overseer to take a man's child from him permanently because the man was temporarily on relief following a disastrous flood.[44] In Seventeenth Century England paupers were required to wear badges in the same way as Jews were required to do in Nazi Germany.[45] The settlement laws applied largely to the poor. Adam Smith wrote in 1776, "There is scarce a poor man in England of forty years of age. . .who has not in some part of his life felt himself cruelly oppressed by this ill-contrived law of settlement."[46] Piven and Cloward express it thus:

> Laborers could not organize, they could not refuse work, they could not exploit labor shortages to demand higher wages, and they could not move to new localities to find better working conditions.[47]

But the poor man who could not work could be sent back to his settlement on the mere suspicion of him becoming indigent.

Supervision and Control

The fourth method was perhaps, in the long run, the most degrading. Because the money on which they lived was not theirs to begin with they had to put up with whatever conditions and demands for behavior their masters liked to impose on them. The British Act of 1834 was avowedly:

> based on the principle that no one should be suffered to perish through want of what is necessary for sustaining life, but, at the same time, that if he is to be supported at the expense of the public, he must be content to receive such support on the terms deemed most consistent with the general welfare.[48]

These terms may be as reasonable as requirements to attend clinics for one's rehabilitation, or as draconian as being forbidden to marry or having one's children taken from one with no due process involved, as was possible in Denmark for certain families as late as 1947.[49]

This kind of social control may require a higher standard of morality than is enforced on the population as a whole. Its most general form, however, is supervision by some public official. Karl and Elizabeth De Schweinitz say that:

> For better or worse many of those who are responsible for the administration of law or services, or who are interested in social reforms, or in advancing their own private advantage, want to subject the welfare recipient to a double standard – to law, requirements, and propaganda, as they affect the whole community of which he is a member and then to a special impact from the public assistance worker.[50]

Lewis Merriam argued that Social Security, as it was established in the United States, was a form of relief because it was not actuarial (one could receive from it more than a strict actuarial insurance would pay). He says that of those found "reasonably competent to manage their own affairs:"

> It is not contended that they should have as much freedom in handling the money that comes to them from the public treasury as they have in handling the resources that they

have earned by their own efforts. The receipt of funds collected through taxation gives the state a right to supervise . . .but this right should be sparingly exercised. . .

but for those "whose needs result in part from their inability to handle their own affairs:"

the recipients of the benefits should be subject to the supervision of competent, professionally trained, public employees, and payments should be contingent upon suitable use and application of the public funds provided.[51]

These, although we have strayed far from the original Puritans, are concepts directly attributable to the world-view, or theology, or heresy, whichever one likes to call it, that began with them and not only persists but is on the ascendent in society today.

The Capitalist-Puritan Religion

A Pervasive View

This view of society, and of the nature of man, is one of the three basic "religions" of the Western World. It is not confined to America, although it seems to prosper there most, nor to Protestantism, although in its extreme form it is most often found among people who claim to be Protestant. Within that welter of denominations and sects it is not confined to those labeled "fundamentalist," although again, its more extreme forms tend to be associated with fundamentalism. It is not confined to those who proclaim a religious faith, although it appears in a slightly different form where it derives from, or is applied to, basically capitalistic or religious matters. It is part of everyone's heritage in this culture, whether the person claims to be a liberal, a humanist, or an orthodox Christian free from the heresy involved. It is sometimes associated with "Americanism" or "Conservatism."

At the moment it is being enunciated more clearly than it has been for many years. It varies very little from generation to generation, which is perhaps the mark of a true religion; social conditions, although they may have played a part in its original formulation, seem to have little effect on its basic beliefs. In its thinking about the poor, the technologically unemployed, and the deserted mother are not treated essentially differently from the "rogues and vagabonds" of the Sixteenth Century.

Basic Assumptions

Much of what the pervasive view of society believes is implicit and is only enunciated by extremists, either in capitalism or in religion. Many people would be shocked if they were forced to look at its basic suppositions; yet they act instinctively on them. Let us look briefly at what these are.

1. That humankind, with the exception perhaps of oneself or one's own kind, is basically evil, and if left to themselves, people will lie, cheat, steal, and take advantage of others. They must be restrained from these activities by those who, for some reason, are believed to be free of these proclivities, whether these be the elect (in a purely religious context), or the upper classes, or the successful, or simply those in power. Indeed it is a moral duty of the "sahibs" to do this restraining; anything else is "permissiveness" and immoral. (Where children are concerned the "sahibs" are their "elders and betters.")

2. Certain sins are seen to be particularly heinous. This is not the old Catholic distinction between "mortal" and "venial" sins, but the selection of certain sins, largely culturally determined, although often given divine sanction for this selection. They are also usually sins that threaten property or have economic consequences. Although lust has retained its pride of place, despite Jesus' extraordinarily gentle handling of it, [52] the unwillingness to work did not become a major sin until the economy needed a class of people willing to work at anything their masters wanted them to, [53] nor was intemperance a major sin until the distillation of gin made it possible for the poor to get drunk extremely cheaply and thus be unavailable both for work and for conversion. [54] Neither have more than almost casual authority for their selection from the Bible; one has to "hunt texts" to establish them as major prohibitions, [55] while the sins which the Bible does emphasize again and again are almost ignored, specifically pride, avarice, injustice, and idolatry, or worshipping Mannon rather than God. Disrespect for authority does appear in the Ten Commandments, and in Proverbs and Paul's letter, but is not mentioned in the Gospels.

3. The major purpose in life is to "get ahead," succeed, and in particular, acquire material things. This is done in competition with one another. The people who "get ahead" are those of whom society approves and who have earned the right to be masters. They are the "good" people, and in religious circles are those favored by God. They get ahead, however, not so much by doing God's will as by obeying the laws of capitalist economics, which are seen as having been built into the universe in some inexorable way and are neglected at one's peril. Sometimes, it

it true, the purpose of life is stated to be "saved" and thus assured of Heaven. This, by itself, is not a sign of puritan-capitalism and can lead to a life of service and even self-imposed poverty; it becomes capitalist-puritan where it is associated with worldly success or is the basis of a desire to control the lives of others.

4. Persons are almost totally responsible for their own success or failure. Failure is an indication of weakness, lack of self-discipline, or insufficient will-power. Persons can, through an act of will, reform themselves and better their conditions. They often, however, require motivating to exercise this will.

5. The principal means of motivating someone are exhortation, shaming, and punishment. Rewards may play some part in this, especially in the form of the "carrot" which lies ahead but is not actually bestowed; but one should be careful not to reward someone for doing what he or she should be doing in the first place.[56] Sympathy with a person who has failed, and this usually includes empathy [57] as well, is seen as condoning unacceptable behavior and leaving him or her no motivation to change. It is to "pamper" or "indulge." "Discipline," a favorite word, consists almost entirely in punishments, which are often retributive in nature. Belief in corporal punishment and the death penalty are common in this system.

6. The major purpose of government is the maintenance of law and order, the protection of property, and the assurance that everyone shall receive what he or she "deserves" and no one what he or does not "deserve." Government should not interfere more than is minimally necessary in the economic system or in culturally approved activities, even if these should threaten the general welfare or the rights of a minority group in the population. It should, however, legislate against most forms of deviancy or anything considered sinful.

This is perhaps an overdrawn picture, although it can be substantiated. Not everyone whose basic beliefs are capitalist-puritan would agree, perhaps, to all of these presuppositions. The problem is rather that most of us agree to some of them and unconsciously, perhaps, apply them in our thinking about the poor.

Evangelicalism and Humanitarianism

Revival

The religious revival of the late Eighteenth and early Nineteenth Centuries should have done something to counteract the rigidities of the capitalist-puritan belief. Some writers believe it did so. Young and Ashton write:

> The sentiment of human benevolence, and its practical expression, derived directly from religious influence. It came from the quickened knowledge, born of the new religious revivalism, that all men were children of God, and loved by Him. It began to mean, as the century advanced, that all men had equal dignity in the eyes of God, and therefore should be so regarded by other men.[58]

Richard Niebuhr adds that it "was responsible for creating a considerable sentiment for greater democracy among many of the wealthier citizens of the nation."[59] Trevelyan speaks of a better relationship between the middle-classes and the poor, but puts this down to economic factors: a common front against the oppression of the landlord class.[60]

And in some ways things did get better. Despite repressive efforts such as Peterloo and the savage treatment of the agricultural laborers' "revolt" of 1830,[61] in England the Reform Bill was passed, the Corn Laws were repealed, and the franchise extended. The poor found champions in Cobden, Bright, and Lord Shaftsbury.[62] *Oliver Twist* and later Kingsley's *Water Babies* illustrated the plight of the poor and in 1851 Henry Mayhew completed his monumental study of "the sufferings, and frequent heroism under those sufferings of the poor" in which he hoped,

> to bestir those in high places. . .to improve the condition of a people whose misery, ignorance and vice, amidst all the immense wealth and great knowledge of the first city in the world is, to say the least, a national disgrace.[63]

Poor Law Reform Act

Yet, only two years after the passage of the Reform Act, the British Parliament passed the Poor Law Reform Act of 1834, with its virtual abolition of outdoor relief (cash or in-kind assistance allowing people to remain in their own homes). Trevelyan praises the "social organization" involved, and says that the national and centralized character of the new Poor Law "made it easier to carry out the alleviations and improvements on which later public opinion insisted,"[64] but he also comments that:

> When outdoor relief was the means of livelihood to many thousands in town and country, it was terrible to cut it off

all at one stroke, without at the same time enforcing a living wage, or supplying any shelter for the unemployed and their dependents [other] than the workhouse. . .Even the aged and the sick. . .had not the means to live at home, and yet received no better treatment in the workhouse than if they had come there through their own fault.[65]

Evangelicism and Reform

Paradoxically, in fact, although evangelicism was a religious movement that emphasized love rather than justice,[66] and was essentially individualistic, its actual results were not a further understanding of the plight of the individual, but large-scale reforms that affected in the main the working poor and made the lot of the unproductive poor even harder. Niebuhr suggests two reasons why this happened. In the first place class distinctions were at their height at this time. The old relationship between master and man, which involved mutual respect and mutual interdependence, had broken down under the impact of capitalism and industrialization.[67] Although the working poor and the middle classes had found some common ground, as we have seen, this did not include the upper classes, who made most of the laws, or the unproductive poor, who were the scapegoats for these decisions.

But, more importantly, Evangelicism was not, according to Niebuhr, a true "religion of the disinherited," offering millenarian hopes. Although it appealed to all classes, it remained largely in middle class hands. And as happens all too often, it was selective in its view of sin, and this sin was often of a very personal nature. Not only did it emphasize personal sins such as irreverence and intemperance rather than collective ones such as oppression and injustice (Niebuhr says that Wesley was "more offended by the blasphemous use of the name of God than by the blasphemous use of His creatures)[68] and was more impressed by the vices to which the poor had succumbed than to the evils to which they had been subjected. But the sins of which Evangelicism convicted the rich and the poor were different.[69]

Different Sins

Original sin loses its force as an equalizer if one is subject to very different temptations from those that beset other people. The sin to which one is not prone is seen as unforgiveable, while the sin to which one is prone can without too much difficulty be seen as forgiveable because of the strength of the temptation involved. The most obvious sin of the rich — luxurious living — is by its nature not much of a temptation to the poor, and the most visible sins of the poor (in the eyes of a rich man) – failure to earn his own living – is irrelevant to the rich. One can almost sympathize with the Duchess of Buckingham, who would not say the General Confession, "because it is monstrous to be told that you have a heart as sinful as the common wretches that crawl the earth."[70]

But Evangelicism did do much to correct the notion that the well-to-do were especially favored by God. They were sinful, not in the same way as the poor, it is true, but sinful all the same. Many of them took to heart the problem of the camel and the needle's eye and Wesley's fear of riches. But Wesley's solution was to get all one can, save all one can, and give all one can. Andrew Carnegie is reputed to have said that a man should be embarassed if he dies rich.[71]

Results

In fact the main impact of the Evangelical movement on the rich may have been to restore for a time the prominence of self-fulfillment as a motive for helping others. While not so blatant, perhaps, as in medieval times, the motive is obvious. Of the philanthropy for which the first part of the Nineteenth Century is noted, Young and Ashton say that it "was the bridge in many cases between their business dealings and their Christian conscience."[72]

Niebuhr holds that the socially beneficial results of the Evangelical Movement were never designed, but accrued as by-products of the covenant [73] and that much of the leadership for the new reforms came from other sources, notably the Jews, and was "the only effective substitute for the Christian leadership which had once been unfailingly available for justice but which had died out."[74] However, the next move did in fact come from a Christian source and led to two new developments which were, in great measure, to mold attitudes towards the poor in the years to come.

Chalmers on Charity

Charity and Justice

Thomas Chalmers (1780-1847) is held up as a thorough-going example of Puritan smugness by both Weber and Tawney for his attempt to replace the Poor Law by a system of charity in which the poor would be largely dependent on the compassion of the rich. De Schweinitz also thinks little of him for the same reason. He is reported as specifically condemning any idea that the poor have a "right" to subsistence from the State or from anyone else.[75]

But his objection to public relief was not so much based on a denial of the concept of justice as it was on a belief that justice was not being done. "It is playing fast and loose with a people," he wrote, "first to make a declaration of their right, and then to plant obstacles in the way of their making it good."[76] He also thought that a public system was a mechanical and conscience-saving device that was stifling the impulses of kindliness and compassion in all classes of society. The Poor Law, he thought, "was the cruelest reproach which the government of a country ever laid upon its subject."[77] This criticism is not without merit. Despite the uncertainty and unfairness of a system of private giving, there does seem to be, from my observation, some lessening of a feeling of common responsibility for one's neighbor where Government is assumed to be responsible for meeting everyone's needs.[78]

Valuing Persons

Chalmers indeed restores to charity some of its original meaning, the valuation of the other person. In a world which recognized hard-and-fast class distinctions he could write that "by putting ourselves under the roof of a poor neighbor, we in a manner put ourselves under his protection and render him for a time our superior,"[78] a truly remarkable statement for the time.

In many ways he is like Vives. He worked with a fairly homogeneous and self-dependent population. He divided his parish into wards, as Vives had his cities, each being the responsibility of a deacon, or, in Vives' case, a "prefect." He believed strongly, as did Vives, in the importance of a personal interest, and he coupled it, as did Vives, with a rigorous examination of each applicant's circumstances. These two activities together form what Young and Ashton somewhat surprisingly call "one of the fundamental tenets of all modern casework"[79] but was undoubtedly the forerunner of the Charity Organization movement of the later Nineteenth Century.

Science

What Chalmers added to Vives was that this examination was to be in some way "scientific." How much the work of Chalmer's deacons was in fact scientific is, it might be suggested, open to doubt. There was a good deal of the old moralism about. But the judgment by which, as Aquinas says, pity needs regulation [80] was to be found in the findings of science rather than in the authority of the moral law. Chalmers believed in science. He accepted without question Malthus's theories of population, which he describes as "as unrefragable as the most rigid demonstration" and this led him to demand that the poor, in their own interest, limit their procreative proclivity. In this way, he believed, poverty could be abolished.[81] He was somewhat distressed to find that the poor did not welcome the suggestion.

Intangibles

There is also a second characteristic of Chalmer's work that foreshadowed a future trend. This is the belief that intangible services, those that deal in some way with a person's psyche, are more important than is material aid. As Chalmers puts it, character must come first and comfort second. To a critic who argued that if you give a man a coat he will come to church, Chalmers replied that if a man be induced to come to church, he will want, and get, himself a coat.[82]

While intangible services may be important in helping someone, to elevate them above material help often means ignoring or even despising the latter. This happened, as we shall see, among the Christian Socialists. It is apparent even today. Most social work students want to be "therapists" rather than providers of relief.

While some would argue that "therapy" is a more challenging skill to acquire and deserves a higher status for that reason, when applied to the poor rather than to the mental patient it shows itself not to be free of the belief that to be poor is a result of some lack of character or ability to adjust in the poor person. As Piven and Cloward have it:

> The older philanthropic treatment consisted of a strict regimen of individual surveillance and discipline, the contention being that poverty proved the existence of moral weakness; casework prescribes modern procedures of psycho-social diagnosis, "individualization" and counseling, as if by being poor the client proves his personality weakness and his need for professional treatment.[83]

Jesus and Tangible Services

Jesus' use of Deuteronomy 8:3, or rather the partial statement, "Man does not live by bread alone," is often quoted in support of the primacy of intangible services as if Jesus was condemning bread, despite his asking for it in the Lord's Prayer. In Matthew 25, also, the help given to "the least of these" was of a very practical nature: "I was hungry and you gave me food, I was thirsty and you gave me drink, I was a stranger and you welcomed me. . ." He did not say, "I was in need of counseling. . ." Nor, of course, did he say that man also needed counseling or therapy.

To elevate intangible services over the practical is a heresy, if a somewhat lesser one than the use of alms to ensure one's own salvation or ascribing Original Sin to the poor and Grace only to the successful.

The Four Bases for Judgment

Four Bases for Judging Need

Chalmers' claim to make necessary prudential judgments on the basis of "science"[84] is perhaps of more importance than the support of intangible services. It is a claim that has been made ever since his time, and justifies a digression at this time. There are, in fact, four types of judgment that can be made about the need of someone who is claiming support from someone else or from the community at large. These are, somewhat simplistically:

1. The judgment of the "saint," or what is thought a person deserves.
2. The judgment of the social scientist, or what is believed to be of the most benefit to the person.
3. The judgment of the law, or what it has been declared that the person has a right to.
4. The judgment of the person herself, or what she sees herself as needing.

The Person's Own Judgment

This fourth kind of judgment would hardly be practical if it were applied to individual financial need; nevertheless it was mooted seriously with regard to other services in the late 1960s and early 1970s, under what was known as the "warehouse" theory in which social services were seen as commodities which people should be allowed to order at will.[85] "Indigenous" (poor) expediters or advocates would represent the poor in his or her dealings with relief authorities, largely, however, over matters of misapplication of the law or failure to inform an applicant of his or her rights.[86] The concept, moreover, that the poor should have a voice in determining policy that affect them became important only under President Johnson's "Great Society," with its slogan of "maximum feasible participation" of the poor in policy-making.[87]

Mainly, however, this meant pressure on officials and on the public to exercise their judgments more humanely or more equitably. The final judgments were still made by one of the other three criteria. The saint, the social scientist, or the lawmaker could listen to what the poor saw themselves as needing, and for a time they did so, but they still reserved to themselves the final decisions.

Social Science

The recourse to science rather than to morality seemed at first to be a great improvement. Science has an air about it of the objective and non-judgmental. It can concentrate on what is good for one rather than on condemning one.

And science can be extremely useful in at least two ways. It can tell us the likely results of a policy or a program. A little good economics, for instance, could have shown that the "Speenhamland" system (introduced in England in 1795) of subsidizing wages from the rates, would force down wages. (It is interesting that the more logical system of enforcing a minimum wage was rejected, according to Trevelyan, as "unscientific.")[88] A showing that old people die more quickly when removed from unhygienic but personally preferred conditions and placed in hygienic institutions has done much to change methods of caring for the elderly.

Science, also, has contributed much to empathy: the study of ecological factors associated with child abuse has gone far to dispel the notion that all child-abusers are unnatural monsters; the very discovery of the unconscious has made it plain that not all behavior can be altered by an act of will. To some extent *"tout savoir"* can become *"tout pardonner."*

Yet it makes no very real difference if I am thought of as maladjusted or if I am labeled immoral. I may still be denied my right to live my own life and make my own decision. I am still treated as inferior. Science, when used as a criterion for judgment about another person's needs, rather than as illuminator or a predicter of likely results, is open to just as many perversions as is the moral judgment, and can bear just as hardly on the poor. Let us look at some of the reasons for this.

Value Problems in Social Science

In the first place science, when applied to the human situation, can never by value-free. As Voegelin says of Weber's *wertlose Wissenschaft*

> Such a science would not be in a position to tell anybody whether he should be an economic liberal or a socialist, a democratic constitutionalist, or a Marxist revolutionary, but it could tell him what the consequences would be if he tried to translate the values of his preference into political practice.[89]

One modern philosopher, Erich Fromm, does indeed try to argue that science can create ethical values. He equates Freud's belief that persons progress from an oral through an anal to a genital stage of sexuality with a progression from dependency and greed through meanness to "the mature, independent, productive character" as if this hierarchy of values was confirmed by Freud's theories and therefore given scientific sanction.[90] But what he ignores is the question whether, even if people normally go through this progression according to Freud, they should in fact do so. There is some evidence that the so-called "genital character" is aggressive and prone to violence and therefore may be not so desirable and that perhaps a state of ungenitalized "polymorphous perversion" might be preferable. This might, in fact, be one of the lessons of the Fall.

The chief problem, however, with the values that are inherent whenever social science is applied to persons is that the values themselves cannot be examined by any scientific method. They have no real, measurable existence. The "saint" did at least have some authority, in his theology, for the values by which he judged others. The scientist has only his personal preference or a sort of general assumption that there is some sort of consensus in society about what is desirable. And these are generally rather crude statements.

Limits of Empiricism

Moreover, when the social scientist comes to evaluating results, and therefore making a value-judgment, he can, if he is to remain a scientist, give credit only to those things that can be measured. in fact, he is apt to hold that those things which cannot be measured, and which include the whole existential state of persons, do not exist. As an article puts it, "results that cannot be measured are probably an illusion" and even a showing that satisfaction by a people receiving a service is not permissible as a criterion of its success since such a finding is not replicable.[91] And those results which are measurable are in general behaviors of which society approves or disapproves, such as conformity to norms, financial independence, and "success" rather than more existential values such as liberty, happiness, or self-fulfillment.

In addition, science, by its very nature, stands apart from, or outside of, the object which it is examining. It is forced to describe the object it is examining in terms of its difference from some other object or from some norm which it has developed. This has had two results. The first is a concentration on the degree of deviance from the norm, or maladjustment. If one should imagine that the judgment of the "saint" was devastating, the following quotation from a believer in a scientific approach to people who are in trouble might be considered:

> Sharper social study methods and increased psychiatric knowledge bring us daily more usable information about the uncontrolled impulsivity, the impairment in capacity to form relationships, and the ego and superego defectiveness of those whose social and emotional dysfunctioning comes to our attention.[92]

The Temptation to Control

Humankind, viewed through a magnifying glass, is a pretty sorry creature. One political scientist goes so far as to question the whole premise of democracy on these grounds:

> The findings of personality research show that the individual is a poor judge of his own interest. . .An examination of the total state of the person will frequently show that his theory of his own interests is far removed from the course of procedure which will give him a happy and well adjusted life.[93]

There is therefore a great temptation to control him and "adjust" him for his own good, in accordance with what one believes a "happy and well-adjusted" life to be.

Ironies of Individualism

The second result of the use of an external examination of persons and their condition has been the principle of individualization. Chalmers' "scientific approach" involved careful discrimination between people in terms of their individual situations. At first this may seem a liberating principle. It frees people from stereotypes. It has become in recent years almost an article of faith. Mary Richmond, who introduced the whole concept of individual diagnosis to the practice of social work, calls it "doing different things with different people" and saw it as a test of administrative skill and an advanced stage in the development of democracy.[94]

The United States, which prides itself on its scientific tenor, has the most individualized welfare system in the Western world. There are hundreds of variables in its public assistance laws which affect the amount of an individual's grant. It seems almost churlish to suggest, as does

51

Nicolai Berdyaev, that individualizing people forces man "to find his way out of difficulties through conformism, through adaptation,"[95] or to hear that,

> The excessive individualization of the whole design and process of mean's test aid is fundamentally antithetical to the idea of equality. A system which makes so much depend upon a minute examination of every aspect of the individual's situation nessarily involves personalized judgments by officials and invites arbitrary and whimsical exercises of power. . .renders it impossible for the recipient himself to determine to what he is entitled [and] constitutes the very thing intended to be prevented by the idea of a "government of laws and not of men". . .[96]

There are two problems here. The first is that people have two contradictory desires: to be treated the same as others, and to have their own individual circumstances taken into account. Excessive individualism negates the first. The second is of a more philosophical nature, but none the less important. Individualization, as a scientific process, measures what might be called the difference *from*. It compares people or compares them to a norm. This one is stronger, richer, more fortunate, has less responsibilities, is better situated.

Persons and Objects

But people are more than their difference from others. Each person is unique. She has her own aspirations, her way of coping with life or relating to others, her own definition of happiness. And about this, science as yet can tell us very little, although it sometimes attempts to do so in rather general terms, stating that such and such an experience or environment generally, but not always, will produce such and such a personality. We all, however, know people who transcend or fail to respond to their circumstances. It is conceivably possible that science may someday be able to deal with all the variables that produce personality, but at the moment we are far from any such knowledge. Personality, as we know it, is what really matters. It is what one falls in love with in another. Berdyaev says of it, that it is the:

> freedom and independence of man in relation to nature, to society and the State, but not only is it not egocentric self-affirmation, it is the very opposite.[97]

Science can tell one everything about a person except what makes him or her truly human. Fromm points out the essential relationship between scientific knowledge and really knowing another person. Knowledge in thought, that is, in his thinking psychological knowledge, is a necessary condition for full knowledge in the act of love or in human relationships:

> I have to know the other person and myself objectively, in order to be able to see his reality, or rather, to overcome the illusion, the irrationally distorted picture I have of him. Only if I know a person objectively can I know him in the ultimate essence, in the act of love.[98]

At the same time he believes that the great popularity of psychology indicates an interest in the knowledge of persons but also betrays the funamental lack of love in human relations. It "becomes a substitute for full knowledge in the act of love, instead of being a step towards it.[99]

Walter Lippmann is even more direct:

> The power of the expert depends upon separating himself from those who make the decision, upon not caring, in his expert self, what decision is made. . .When he begins to care too much, he begins to see what he wishes to see, and by that fact ceases to see what he is there to see.[100]

That, of course, depends on what one believes he or she is there to see. Science, in fact, always faces the temptation to see persons as objects rather than subjects of the sentence, and to create what Buber calls "I-It" rather than "I-Thou" relationships.[101] It is true that empathy has been validated scientifically as necessary to helping people,[102] as if we did not know that from other sources. But science can tell us very little about its quality.

Science and ideology

Science also had other problems. It is hard to know what to believe. Anyone who has lived through a cycle of supposedly scientific theories on childrearing knows that things can be presented as scientific fact when in fact the right questions have been asked to support a pre-supposed value. When social workers first decided that early adoptions were good and that one did not have to wait a year or even longer to assure oneself of a child's "adoptability," a rash of articles appeared showing that the psychological tests on which social workers had been relying were in fact highly inaccurate. Which psychologist does one believe: Freud, or Rank, or Jung, or Adler or one of their successors? Science can also be perverted. The Nazis claimed a scientific base for their racial theories. So did many American segregationists.

Admittedly these were pseudo-scientific theories, although many took them as proven truth. But what can we say when two eminent American sociologists, Herbert Spencer and William Graham Sumner, could devise anything so wildly unscientific as Social Darwinism, which equated success in the marketplace with natural selection, and convicted the poor of something not unlike biological inferiority. It might also be remarked that Darwin never suggested that a species that survived was any more desirable than one that perished; only that it was able to survive, and that he wrote about species and not individuals. It is hard to see the social desirability of the adaptability, say, of tetanus germs.

The problem is that science can set no limits on itself. Once one thinks that one knows, and is convinced that one is right, the temptation to try to control others becomes very great. It is not science that is dangerous, but what people can do with it.

Judgment of Law

This leaves the judgment of the law as the least corruptible, perhaps, of the types of judgment. While laws can be corrupt or be perverted by a class or a culture (witness perhaps the Poor Law Reform Act or the Settlement Laws in England, or the "Jim Crow" laws in the United States), and while the law may "be an ass," its imperfections have long been recognized, and to some extent it has been restrained by the safeguards of due procedure and precedent.

It is the accumulated wisdom and foolishness of the last two thousand years, but it has been concerned traditionally with the limitation of the power of the strong over the weak and is as little open as any human form of justice to individual interpretation. But the concept of a legal and enforceable right to assistance under certain circumstances was still a long way in the future in Chalmers' time.

Notes

The Work Ethic and Election

[1] See Chapter 1, note 64.

[2] J. S. Mill, *Principles of Political Economy*, V, xi, p. 13, quoted by Lubbock, *Some Poor Law Questions*, p. 47.

[3] For the economic, rather than the theological explanation see H. M. Robertson, *The Rise of Economic Individualism*, Cambridge, 1933, which is in general a rejoinder to Max Weber, *The Protestant Ethic and the Spirit of Capitalism*, London, 1930.

[4] According to Troeltsch, *The Social Teaching*, p. 555.

[5] Weber, *The Protestant Ethic*, p. 80.

[6] Luther, *Liber Vagatorum, 4,* quoted by de Schweinitz, *England's Road*, p. 37.

[7] Maurice B. Reckitt, *Religion in Social Action, London,* 1937, p. 62.

[8] League of Local Welfare Executives, *The Good Old Days, Richmond. Va., 1950.*

[9] Weber, *The Protestant Ethic*, p. 111.

[10] Ibid., p. 159.

[11] Ibid., p. 122.

[12] R. B. Perry, Puritanism and Democracy, New York, 1944, p. 95.

[13] H. Richard Niebuhr, *The Social Sources*, pp. 80ff.

[14] Ibid., p. 85.

[15] R. H. Tawney, *Religion and the Rise of Capitalism, London* quoted by Niebuhr, *The Social Sources,* p. 87.

[16] Perry, Puritanism and Democracy, p. 95.

[17] See Note 5, Chapter 1.

[18] The Northampton Covenant, quoted by Thomas Jefferson Wertenbaker, *The Puritan Oligarchy*, New York, 1947, Gorsset's Universal Library, p. 58. Curiously enough this book, although advertised as "an account of the whole range of life in the New England colonies," makes no mention of the poor.

[19] Loch, *Charity and Social Life*, p. 303.

[20] Weber, *The Protestant Ethic*, pp. 36-37.

[21] Troelsch, *The Social Teaching,* p. 512.

[22] *Westminster Confession of Faith, XVIII, ii.*

[23] Ibid., XVIII, iii.

[24] Ibid., XVIII, v.

[25] Ibid., XVIII, vii.

[26] *The Westminster Larger Catechism,* Question 96.

[27] Erich Voegelin, *The New Science of Politics*, Chicago, 1952, p. 129.

[28] Ibid., p. 147.

[29] R. V. Holt, The Unitarian Contribution to Social Progress, quoted in A. F. Young and E. T. Ashton, *British Social Work in the Nineteenth Century,* New York, 1956.

[30] Josiah Quincy, *Report on the Poor Law of Massachusetts,* 1821, reproduced by Breckenridge, *Public Welfare . . . Documents*, p. 33.

[31] George Gilder, *Wealth and Poverty*, New York, 1981, p. 118.

[32] Ibid., p. 117.

[33] Samuel Johnson, quoted by Rodgers, *The Cloak of Charity,* p. 18.

[34] Johnson had biblical authority for his remedy. Proverbs 31:6-8, after saying that strong drink is not for Kings, reads:

> Give strong drink to him who is perishing,
> And wine to those in bitter distress,
> Let them drink and forget their poverty
> And remember their misery no more.
> Open your mouth for the dumb,
> For the rights of those who are left desolate.

[35] The best-known exposition is B. F. Skinner's *Beyond Freedom and Dignity.*

Spurring the Poor to Independence

[36] Young and Ashton, *British Social Work*, p. 47.

[37] Masterson, *Chalmers on Charity,* p. 107.

[38] G. M. Trevelyan, *History of England*, London, 1926.

[39] de Schweinitz, *England's Road*, p. 66.

[40] Ibid., p. 92.

[41] *The Report from His Majesty's Commissioners for Inquiring into the Administration and Practical Operation of the Poor Laws*, 1834, quoted by de Schweinitz, *England's Road,* p. 123.

[42] Socialt Tidskrift, *Social Denmark,* Copenhagen, 1947, p. 55.

[43] Edith Abbott, *Public Assistance: American Principles and Policies*, Chicago, 1940, Volume I, p. 127.

[44] J. H. E. Ackley vs. A. A. Tinker, 26 Kan. 485 (1881), reported Ibid., p. 128.

[45] Hubbard, *The Old Book of Wye,* p. 123. Paupers who did not wear their badge – a large Roman "P" in red or blue – could be whipped or deprived of their relief. Nevertheless the churchwardens of Wye had to visit their county town "for a warrant to make the poor wear their badges."

[46] Quoted by de Schweinitz, *England's Road*, p. 43 and Piven and Cloward, *Regulating the Poor*, p. 37.

[47] Piven and Cloward, *Regulating the Poor*, p. 37.

[48] Sir George Nichols, *History of the English Poor Law*, quoted by Lubbock, *Some Poor Relief Questions*, p. 42.

[49] *Social Denmark*, pp. 142-143. There is no intention to single out Denmark here. Many other programs had similar provisions. The Danes are perhaps more explicit about them.

[50] Elizabeth and Karl de Schweintiz, *The Content of the Public Assistance Job*, New York, undated, pp. 9-10.

[51] Lewis, Merriam, *Relief and Social Security*, Washington, 1946, pp. 865-867.

The Capitalist-Puritan Religion

[52] In the story of the woman taken in adultery, John 8:3-11. This is believed by most scholars, however, to be a later interpolation, so one might cite Jesus' acceptance of the woman of Samaria, who was living "in sin," John 4:16-18. Dorothy Sayers, who was asked to speak to the Moral Reform Society of Great Britain, wrote an illuminating pamphlet entitled "The Other Six Deadly Sins," London, 1943.

[53] It is interesting to see how *acedia* is now translated largely as "sloth" and given the meaning of idleness, whereas its original meaning was "dejection," according to the *Encyclopedia of Religion,* edited by Vergilius Ferm, New York, 1945, item on the seven deadly sins, p. 705.

[54] Trevelyan points out that gin was not taxed seriously until 1736, and in the roughly fifty years before this, consumption of it increased more than tenfold. It replaced beer and ale as the staple drink until after this time, when tea became the drink of the poor in England; but in its heyday one could get drunk for a penny. Trevelyan, *History of England* Vol.III, p. 38.

[55] Notably 2 Thessalonians 3:10. There are a numnber of references to strong drink in the Bible, notably Proverbs 9:5, Isaiah 5:11 and 28:1-7 and wine was forbidden to those who had taken certain vows, as well as to John the Baptist (Luke 1:15), but on the other hand we have Proverbs 31:6, Deuteronomy 14:16 and 1 Timothy 5:23.

[56] "Sympathy" and "Empathy" are used here in the sense attributed to them in my *Giving and Taking Help,* Chapel Hill, 1972. "Sympathy" is feeling like someone else, sharing his sorrow, anger or despair; "Empathy" the ability to feel what he is going through or is up against without adopting his attitudes towards the problem.

[58] Young and Ashton, *British Social Work*, p. 41.

[59] Niebuhr, *The Social Sources*, pp. 64-65.

[60] Trevelyan, *History of England*, Volume III, pp. 157 and 187.

[61] In the first of these a peaceful "but orderly" concourse of working men and women was fired on by the militia: a dozen were killed and hundreds injured (Trevelyan, p. 161). In the latter, eleven years later, "the starving agricultural laborers rioted but shed no blood and destroyed little property" but leaders were hanged and 450 of the rank and file transported to Australia leaving their families behind (Trevelyan, p. 177, note).

[62] Who is still celebrated in an English ballad as "an honest and a good man to the poor."

[63] Henry Mayhew, *London Labour and the London Poor*, London 1861-1862, quoted by Allison Lockwood, "The Street People of London, 1851," *British Heritage*, 3, 2 (February-March 1982): 24. The passage does not occur in *Mayhew's London*, an abridged but lengthy edition, edited by Peter Quenell (London, 1984), but there is much in this book of interest.

[64] Trevelyan, *History of England*, Volume III, p. 186.

[65] Ibid., p. 185.

[66] Niebuhr, *The Social Sources*, p. 69.

[67] Ibid., pp. 56-57.

[68] Ibid., p .67.

[69] In 1965 I was asked to write an article on the question, "Does Public Welfare Cause Immorality?" the issue being the supposed subsidization of illegitimate births by the Aid to Families with Dependent Children Program. Besides pointing out that at that time only one illegitimate child in ten received relief, I pointed out that even if it were possible to convict welfare clients of lust and sloth (in its modern meaning), which I doubted, I would hate to have to compare them with an average Chamber of Commerce on pride and avarice. *Presbyterian Survey*, 55, 9 (September 1965): 30-32.

[70] Quoted by Niebuhr, *The Social Sources*, p. 61.

[71] According to Smylie, "Gilder, Gilt and the Needle's eye," *Presbyterian Outlook, 164, 4 (April 25, 1982): 6.*

[72] Young and Ashton, *British Social Work*, p. 29.

[73] Niebuhr, *The Social Sources*, p. 66.

[74] Ibid., p. 75

Chalmers on Charity

[75] See Young and Ashton, *British Social Work*, pp. 28-29.

[76] Masterson, *Chalmers on Charity*, p. 106.

[77] Ibid., p. 92.

[78] I cannot substantiate this from any valid study. It has been suggested to me by responsible people in Great Britain, new Zealand, and Sweden. Richard Titmuss, in his *Essays on the Welfare State*, London, 1958, quotes B. De Jouvenal as reporting a "precipitous decline" in voluntary services (*The Ethics of Redistribution*, London, 1951) but does not consider the statement justified.

[79] *Chalmers on Charity*, p. 228.

[80] Young and Ashton, *British Social Work*, p. 78.

[81] *Summa Theologica*, II-II, Question 30.

[82] *Chalmers on Charity*, p. 124.

[83] Ibid., pp. 121-122.

[84] Piven and Cloward, *Regulating the Poor*, p. 177.

The Four Bases for Judgment

[85] It should be clear that judgments of this sort do have to be made: "judgment" should not be confused with "judgmentalism" which is the tendency to make generally negative judgments on others as to their character or rights.

[86] The term was certainly used in practice. I have not, however, been able to find it in the professional literature except in my own "Philosophies of Public Service," *Public Welfare*, 31, 1 (Winter, 1973): 21-25.

[87] There is a good description of this process in Piven and Cloward, *Regulating the Poor*, pp. 296-300.

[88] See discussion of this, ibid., pp. 268-273.

[89] Trevelyan, *History of England*, Volume III, p. 110.

[90] Voegelin, *New Science of Politics*, p. 14.

[91] Erich Fromm, *Man for Himself: An Enquiry into the Psychology of Ethics*, New York, 1947, p. 36.

[92] Edward Newman and Jerry Turem, "The Crisis of Accountability," *Social Work*, 19, 1 (January 1974): 16. See, however, Paul Halmos on "The Mirage of Results," in *The Faith of the Counsellors*, pp. 146-156.

[93] Ruth Ellen Lindenberg, "Hard to Reach: Client or Casework Agency," *Social Work*, 3, 4, (October 1958): 29. It is curious that this statement should be used in an article which lays the principal blame for lack of service on the agency and not on the client.

[94] H. D. Laswell, *Psychopathology and Politics*, New York, 1930, p. 194.

[95] Mary Richmond, *Social Diagnosis*, New York, 1917, pp. 367-368.

[96] Nicolai Berdyaev, *Slavery and Freedom*, translated by R. M. French, Scribner edition, New York, 1944, p. 36.

[97] Jacobus tenBroek and Richard B. Wilson, "Public Assistance and Social Insurance: a Normative Evaluation," U.C.L.A. Law Review, 1 (1954): 265-266.

[98] Berdyaev, *Slavery and Freedom*,, pp. 35-36.

[99] Erich Fromm, *The Art of Loving*, New York, 1956, Bantam Edition, 1963, p. 26.

[100] Ibid., p. 26, note.

[101] Walter Lippmann, *Public Opinion*, New York, 1922, p. 382.

[102] Martin Buber, *I and Thou*, translated by Ronald Gregor Smith, London, 1937.

[103] See, for instance, Robert R. Carkhuff, *Helping and Human Relations*, two volumes, New York, 1969.

TOWARD PROFESSIONALISM: THE NINETEENTH CENTURY TO MARY RICHMOND

The Humanist-Positivist-Utopian Belief

An Emerging Cluster of Views

Chalmers, in fact, stands at the very beginning of a system of beliefs which still dominates thought in America today and which might be called Humanist, Positivist, and Utopian, or HPU for short. It co-exists with the capitalist-puritan belief. Most of us take some assumptions from one and some from the other. It has three roots, or perhaps only two, its Utopianism being perhaps an offshoot of its Humanism. It is not always internally consistent.

Lieby calls the "intellectual history" of the later nineteenth century with regard to the poor, "a great confusion in which social Darwinists and romantic utopians who held contradictory views could both find a wide appeal."[1] He quotes Amos Warner, who wrote in 1894, as saying that there was a dialectic between "philanthropists" who believed that something must be done to help the needy and "economists" who believed that a policy must follow the best scientific understanding of human affairs.[2] He writes of the "astonishing growth of private philanthropy" of that time, which, he says, "revealed that the most sentimental sort of charity still moved rich and poor."[3] He ascribes this to evangelical Protestants, Catholics, and Jews, who "held that one mission of the church was to help the forlorn and defeated, never mind the godless Darwinists or liberal economics, and, quite apart from formal religion, the democratic ethos was solicitous about humble people."[4]

That last phrase is, I think, significant, for I would suggest that it was not so much the original impulse to charity in response to God's love as it was the general humanitarianism, which is the first stage in humanism, that actuated both the churches and the agnostics. It was that "sentimental" charity which, as Reinhold Niebuhr has pointed out, can only be corrected by the insights of religion.[5]

Humanism

The initial impact of humanism is to ascribe great worth to humankind. In fact, the first article of belief in the Humanist-Positivist-Utopian creed is that persons are basically good. In its more positivistic mood it may assert that "man is amoral and asocial at birth"[6] (it has to deny Original Sin) and that "all human behavior is the result of interaction between the biological organism and its environment."[7] But it starts from the premise of Rousseau that "man is born free, but everywhere he is in chains." It must believe in man and his perfectibility. This may not be strictly scientific. Halmos points out how psychiatrists, who are usually HPU-ists, believed in the triumph of love over hatred, despite Freud's assertion that they were evenly balanced. It can be shown that in America, at least, the optimistic earlier Freud of the oral-anal-genital progression was accepted in place of the later Freud of the death-wish.[9] But, even if he is not born "good," man must be able to be made so, and this is generally to be achieved by freeing him to "be himself."

This is where the work of Voegelin's "Gnostics" begins. Each has a different solution for humankind's dilemma. With Freud, the early Freud at least, the key was the removal of repressions imposed by society. With Marx it was the re-ordering of the economic system, with Dewey proper education, with Skinner the reinforcing of positive behavior and the discouragement of the negative. If these corrections are made, the persons' needs are therefore fulfilled; they will attain a state that is variously described, according to the vocabulary used, as goodness, maturity, adjustment, or productivity, in which most of their and society's problems would be resolved. Society, although presently the cause of persons' failures to reach their potential, exists, or should exist, to fulfill their needs, both material and emotional.

Moreover, this fulfillment is in general thought bound to occur. One cannot but be impressed that most histories of welfare describe a general amelioration of conditions throughout the centuries. The HPU-ist must believe in progress, or a generally lineal nature, although he or she may believe in something of a Hegelian dialectic with a generally upward trend. It was not until after the First World War raised questions about the progress of humanity that we get "anti-Utopias" such as Huxley's *Brave New World*, and after the Second World War Orwell's *1984*. The utopias of the latter Nineteenth Century are all optimistic: William Morris' *News from Nowhere*, Edward Bellamy's *Looking Backward*, and Charles Sheldon's *In His Steps*.[10]

Contrasts

Succinctly, the differences between the Humanist-Positivist-Utopian (HPU) belief and that of Capitalist-Puritanism (CP) can be listed as follows:

1. CP thought holds humanity to be basically evil; HPU thought, basically good.

2. The major purpose of life, in the CP creed, is to get ahead; in the HPU it is to fulfill oneself or achieve one's potential.[11]

3. In the CP set of beliefs, persons are almost totally responsible for their own condition; in HPU thought they are the product of forces acting on them, whether these be external or internal.

4. The purpose of society is, in the CP view, the maintenance of order and the protection of economic rights; in HPU thought the rights involved are those of opportunity and freedom from restraint and the purpose of society is to enable persons to fulfill their "basic" needs.[12]

5. The way to achieve a more perfect society is, in CP thought, largely a matter of discipling society's errant members, although rewards and exhortation have their place; in HPU thinking it is either, or rather both, re-structuring society's laws and policies and treating the individual in a scientific manner.

6. In the CP system, values are thought to be absolute, often derived from Holy Writ, although, as we have seen, they are often selective in terms of cultural and economic preferences, and include such beliefs as those of capitalist economics. In the HPU framework, values tend to be relative, although they are in general inherited from the Judeo-Christian tradition. They have, however, been severed from these roots and may be explained as necessary to social co-operation, or, by the sociobiologists, to the preservation of the species. More generally they are simply assumed, or are those favored by the culture, which renders them liable to change as the culture changes.

7. CP thought sees the only hope, other than God's establishment of the Millenium, to lie in the moral reformation of each individual and has some doubts about that. HPU thought is much more confident that humanity, through science, can and will accomplish Utopia. This will be the job of the social scientists. As science advances, so will persons and society. There is, however, one other difference. CP tends to look backwards to some imagined age of greater innocence, while to the HPU-ist progress is always being made, and the newest is usually thought best. Gordon Hamilton said in 1941 that "the social sciences allied with the physical sciences must increasingly throw light on social needs and social improvement."[13] In an article of that time one can find something very like Comte's Law of Three Stages, in the

form of a progression from the counseling of the Catholic priest, to that of the Protestant minister, to non-analytical counseling to counseling by means of the newer analytical disciplines, which at that time were believed to be the most scientific.[14]

Humanism and Control

Humanist-Positivist-Utopian doctrines certainly look at first sight to be much more humane, much more reasonable, and in fact much more "Christian" in the commonly used sense of that term than those of Capitalist-Puritanism, and may in fact be considered by some a necessary corrective to them. Undoubtedly HPU-ists have a far better humanitarian record than have CPs, and this has led some HPU-ists to reject any and all religion. Bisno, in his compendium of social work statements in the 1950s, takes issue with what he believes to be religious principles in six of his eight assumptions about the nature of the individual, but his concept of religion is that it is Capitalist-Puritan or, in the case of Catholics, Thomistic.[15]

But humanism has one fatal flaw. That lies in its unrealistic belief that persons are basically good and, if freed from the constraints that society or the environment places on them, will cooperate with others and live in peace with little need for external controls. The problem is simply that when the necessary adjustments in the environment have been made, many people fail to cooperate. These people are then declared to be sick or to be under the influence of persons outside the culture, and they have to be re-educated or controlled. The result is the exact opposite of what was at first intended.

As an English writer put it more than fifty years ago:

this bouyant attitude which built its confidence on belief in Man, certain that he needed God no longer, has ended in such a disbelief in Man, such radical distrust in human nature, that the world is half-paralyzed by reason of it.[16]

The clearest example of this process is probably what has happened to Communism. Granted that true Communism has not, in the view of its apologists, yet been attained (it is at least taking an unconscionably long time in arriving), Marx prophesied that in a communist economy the state would wither away. Man would not need external controls.

Re-reading some of the manifestos of the Russian revolution, one glimpses the promise of a truly free society. The proposals for a peace conference to follow the first World War, put forward by the Central

Executive Committee of the Soviets of Workers' and Soldiers' Deputies (the Tsay-ee-kah) included the "right of self-determination" of all peoples, including the Lithuanians, Latvians, Polish, and Jews in Rumania, that country being compelled to recognize Jews as citizens.[17] Secret diplomacy was to be abolished and in Russia itself education was thought of as something that "neither the government nor the intellectuals nor any power outside of themselves can give" to people. "There is no more superb or beautiful phenomenon that the one of which our nearest descendants will be both witnesses and participants; the building by collective Labour of its own general, rich and free soul."[18]

Yet today the Russian state is far from withering away; the "self-determination" of Letts, Lithuanians, and Poles is virtually non-existent, Anti-Semitism is believed to be rife, and education has become indoctrination.

The Dignity and Worth of the Individual

Nothing so violent has, of course, occurred in the American scene. Nevertheless, the same process exists and can lead us in the direction something not unlike *Brave New World* and *1984*. It has been held in check largely because of values inherited from the Judeo-Christian tradition, chief of which, among social workers today, is the dignity and worth of the individual.[19] This has caused some writers to emphasize the contribution of religion to the social work scene.[20]

But the humanist's belief in the worth and dignity of every individual is not derived from the Christian assertion of God's love for all persons. It is rather a reflection of the humanists that persons are essentially good. Persons are worthy, not because God loves them and has redeemed them, but by virtue of what they are. This is somewhat questionable philosophically and empirically, as well as religiously. F. R. Barry puts it this way:

> . . . it is the faith that there is that in Man, once set free from unfavorable circumstances, which has the power to rise triumphantly to a new and more splendid social order. And this, despite the religious language and the doubtless sincere religious feeling with which its prophets and priests have invested it cannot be held to be genuinely religious. It is in effect the belief that human life is self-sustaining and self-redeeming.[21]

But Berdyaev has the final word. "The error of humanism," he writes, certainly did not lie in the fact that it laid too great an emphasis upon man . . . but in the fact that it did not carry its affirmation of man through to the end, that it could not guarantee the independence of man from the world, and included within itself a danger of enslaving man to society and nature.[22]

It might also be remarked that according to Genesis it was in Paradise itself that humanity first got into serious trouble

The Settlement Movement

Help and Uplift

That Humanist-Positivist beliefs did at first team up, as it were, with the Evangelical Movement, so that Evangelism and Enlightenment worked together, is obvious in what began to be done in the Nineteenth Century. There was a great deal more interest in the condition of the poor. This took various forms. One, which was primarily humanitarian but had a strong religious base, consisted largely in the founding of "missions" in poor neighborhoods, which eventually led to the settlement house movement. There was generally something of a double motive. Part of the motive was genuine concern about the conditions under which the poor were compelled to live and part was a desire to reform the character of the poor. This can be seen in the statement already quoted that recommends both awakening and moral sense and approaching the poor with kindness and an "ingenuous concern for their welfare."[23] Poverty and vice were still thought to go together. But much was truly humanitarian, and we find a writer noting the

> deterioration of the physique of those born in close rooms, brought up in narrow streets, and early made familiar with vice. It was noticed that among the crowds who applied for relief there were few who seemed healthy or were strongly grown.[24]

Personal Encounter

What the settlement workers did was to meet the poor first-hand. Young, idealistic middle-class people, often students from the universities and theological colleges, went and lived among the poor.[25] Jane Addams, perhaps the most famous of settlement workers, herself admitted that Hull House probably did more for the residents than for the people it served directly. "The sheltered and well-brought up young Americans," she wrote in 1893,

> ... reared on the ideal of social justice and on Protestant moral imperatives, had grown uncomfortable about their own sincerity, troubled about their uselessness and restless about being shut off from the common labor by which they lived and which is a great source of moral and physical health.[26]

Allen F. Davis also comments:

> Perhaps the most important contribution by the settlements to the movement for social justice was their effect on the many young men and women who spent a year or two at a settlement and had their minds changed and their visions altered by the experience.[27]

He mentions in particular Harry Hopkins and Frances Perkins, two of the architects of the New Deal.

On a much larger scale, the same thing happened in England during the Second World War, when the enforced encounter between the poor and the middle-class, largely due to the evacuation of poor children and their mothers to the country, so shocked middle-classes that they were ready to accept the National Health Service and the rest of the Beveridge Plan.

The movement was a middle-class movement which included a good deal of "uplift" in terms of art classes and lectures. As one contemporary writer put it, the settlement resident "comes to his study and his work with a stirring belief in the life-giving quality of culture."[28] Some critics, even at that time, complained that the young university students were not really sharing the hardships of the poor. "How could (the university students) advise," wrote one, "how could they confer, how could they pretend to help the family across the way when the conditions under which they were living were so different, when they were not on the same economic basis at all?"[29] But there was real concern for the poor and often appreciation of their qualities.

Knowledge

But what the settlement movement did, more than anything, was to provide the first reliable knowledge about the economic and social conditions in the cities. Science here was being put to what is perhaps its most useful work, examining broad problems, rather than being used as a means of judging the individual. Jane Addams comes near to making this distinction. Although she took pride in the sociological studies that were made at Hull House, she was doubtful about science applied to the individual. To her, this "science" was not scientific enough. A man, she wrote,

> who would hesitate to pronounce an opinion upon the stones lying by the wayside . . . will, without a moment's hesitation, dogmatize about the delicate problems of human conduct . . .[30]

She thought it a sign of the "pseudo-scientific spirit" that the science she saw around her tended to lay stress on negative factors.[31]

Causes of Poverty

There was, however, a great deal of interest in re-examining the causes of poverty. Although there was still some tendency to divide the poor into the worthy and unworthy, there was a beginning emphasis on environmental factors.

Robert Treat Paine identified, in 1893, what he believed to be "four great causes" of pauperism. They are a curious mixture. The first of all is "foul homes" -- a factor that had already been identified as early as 1845 by a medical doctor in America.[32] Although he brackets it with "intoxicating drink," he calls poor housing "a supreme yet eradicable cause of pauperism" and adds that

> the agency which must be invoked to rescue the very poor, whether virtuous or struggling, or degraded and indifferent, is the municipal power to destroy utterly unfit abodes of habitation.[33]

Amos G. Warner, in 1889, makes the distinction between "subjective" and "objective" causes of poverty. Among the former he includes "under-vitalisation" which we might nowadays see as a result of the latter. As causes of undervitalisation he includes industrial conditions and defective sanitation. He points out the difficulty of assessing a "subjective" or an "objective" cause to any particular case -- if a man gets drunk and breaks his leg is it intemperance or an accident? -- and points out the effects of bias in the observer.[34] Nevertheless, in a later article, he produces a table of the causes of poverty in American cities by national background. His table shows only 25% of poverty due to various "misconducts." The causes he finds most prevalent are sickness or death in the family and under-employment, each rather more than a fifth of the whole, and drink, about a sixth.[35]

Social Reform
The workers in settlements, however, were not interested in applying their knowledge to individuals as much as they were in trying to reform the conditions under which most of the poor were living. As Davis has it:

> Because they actually lived in a dreary section of a large city, the settlement residents saw problems from a fresh and different perspective, and they often became initiators and organizers of reform.[36]

Their particular targets were child labor, the working conditions of women, and the right of labor to organize. In promoting these they were, on the whole, very successful, although the Child Labor Amendment finally failed to pass. But the federal Children's Bureau was their creation, and was headed in turn by two of their number. Indirectly, they influenced not only the formulators of the Social Security Act and the Labor Relations Act, but labor leaders like Sydney Hillman and even so influential a man as John Dewey.[37] This they were able to do because they were most often women – good women, educated women, and patrician women, "the first generation of college-women" who "were moderately well-to-do and who for the most part had had a religious upbringing,"[38] in Jane Addams' case, that of a Quaker. They also had their statistics ready to submit. Many of them took part in politics directly. They ran for office and were appointed to boards.

Paternalism

The Concept of Paternalism
The settlement movement took place in an era of paternalism, which went much farther than the relationship between the poor and the well-to-do. It appeared in industrial relations and in company towns. It appeared in international relations, in Kipling's "White Man's burden," and in the United States' treatment of the Philippines and Puerto Rico. It was apparent in many racial relationships in the South, despite Jim Crow

Laws. It occurred in education, in John Dewey, and in Montessori's "civilized child."

Its most obvious manifestation in social welfare was in the Juvenile Courts. The ancient British concept of chancery was revived, but instead of being entrusted to the Lord Chancellor, who was often the country's leading lawyer and one of its leading churchmen, it was put in the hands of anyone who could be elected juvenile judge. The state was seen as *parens patriae* (the Fatherer of all), so in the hands of elected judges, who were often without legal training[39], the power of a parent could be exercised almost at will. "The powers of the Star Chamber were a trifle compared with those of our juvenile courts and courts of domestic relations," writes Roscoe Pound.[40] One state supreme court wrote:

> To save a child from being a criminal . . . the legislature surely may provide for the salvation of such a child . . . by bringing it into one of the courts of the State without any process at all . . . The act is but the exercise by the state of its supreme power over the welfare of its children under which it can take a child from its father and let it go where it will . . . if the welfare of the child . . . can be thus best promoted.[41]

Early books on the Juvenile Court are full of descriptions of the wise, fatherly judge with an arm around the child's shoulders, reasoning with him.[42]

It is true that science was invoked. An early writer describes the court as:

> legal tribunal where law and science, especially the science of medicine and those sciences which deal with human behavior, such as biology, sociology, and psychology, work side by side.[43]

But the result was all too often that of a judge or a social worker "imposing his own particular brand of culture and morals on indigent people."[44]

The Humanist-Positivist-Utopian Link

Roscoe Pound saw the paternalism of the court as a reaction against the mechanical justice of the times and a swing of the pendulum towards judicial discretion after a long period of the rule of law.[45] However, it seems to me that it was only part of what might be called the first stage of Humanist-Positivist-Utopian thought.

While it is true that *parens patriae* referred only to children, the rights of adults were certainly involved. What one can see is the belief that the average wise man, fortified by science, knows what is good and that the delinquent is basically good but is being held back by a poor environment or lack of education or understanding. It assumes that the culture of the upper or middle classes is good and will be adopted by the poor and the deviant when they see its reasonableness. It assumes progress. It is generally humane, not given to blaming people.

Jane Addams in her critique of relief-giving shows great understanding when she praises the mother who, although she is on relief, spends money on games for her children, and reminds us that "man had games long before he cared for a house or for regular meals."[46] She also speaks of "the love and patience which minister to need irrespective of worth."[47]

If one acts out of *noblesse oblige* as the settlement visitors were doing, one is in a sense dealing with children whose faults can be overlooked or better still corrected. One can warn against patronizing the poor – a writer in 1879 says that:

> any notion of condescension or patronage is not only wrong in itself but it is also sure to do harm, by preventing the visitor from getting into right and natural relations with her poor friends.[48]

Or one can maintain, as did Jane Addams, that she was not living in a working-class neighborhood to help the poor but to implement the "theory that the dependence of classes on each other is reciprocal."[49] And many of the workers were truly horrified at the conditions under which the poor were forced to exist. Nonetheless, there is still the assumption that middle and upperclass people have the truth and are superior people. A contemporary writer says of the child-rearing of the poor:

> The children get their correction by a blow today, a laugh tomorrow. Nothing is regular. The truth is never told. The children lie without any consciousness of what the truth is ... The adults, even the older boys and girls, are beyond much help ... A child of ten ... will be ... a different man or woman because for ten years he or she has seen

women for all that time who keep their word, speak the truth, are gentle, kind and unselfish, and are always ready to help.[50]

Nevertheless, it was out of this movement that justice, as a means of treating the needs of the poor, began to be considered again.

The "Christian Socialists" and the Friendly Visitors

Moral Elevation vs. Material Relief

Many settlements had their origin in religious missions of various kinds. Out of these grew, in England, the work of the "Christian Socialists" and, in America, the Association for Improving the Condition of the Poor (AICP), with its concept of "friendly visiting." Although the workers did much to bring the conditions of the poor to the public notice, and, in many cases, the way that the poor were treated in workhouses and hospitals, their primary interest was in the individual poor.

Some of the advice given to the visitors shows a real understanding of what might be called the helping process. One clergyman, for instance, stresses the importance of "looking below the surface of things," courtesy, small caseloads, knowledge of community resources and of the legal rights of tenants and others, fostering interpersonal and interfamilial relations, purposiveness in interviewing, and the paying of "fair business-like rates for any employment offered."[51]

But there was a settled conviction that what the poor needed was the "influence" of the visitor and not material relief. A person who received relief was a "pauper" and not in "honest poverty." The same clergyman who gave the advice above speaks of "how great the gulf" is between the two[52] and states that the "want of money is not the worst evil with which the poor have to contend; it is in most cases but a symptom of other and more important wants."[53]

Indeed, several of the most prominent Christian Socialists seemed to think that there was no need for material relief. Edward Denison, one of the leaders of the Christian Socialists (of whom it was said that "the poor soon came to understand the man who was as liberal with his sympathy as he was chary of meat and coal tickets) said, "I am beginning seriously to believe that all bodily aid to the poor is a mistake."[54] Octavia Hill, one of the movement's outstanding characters, with a great interest in housing, said that she could not see why old age pensions were needed because elderly people could provide for themselves, or their children could provide for them.[55]

Part of this feeling was religious. It was Chalmer's heresy that "spiritual" things were much more important than material. Man, said one speaker at the National Conference of Charities and Corrections, "is a spiritual being, and, if he is to be helped, it must be by spiritual means."[56] But part was the old Puritan belief in the essential depravity of the poor. The same speaker came out strongly for a stigma to be placed on anyone receiving public or private relief and for relief only inside the doors of an institution, where

> cure and education should be the primary objects aimed at
> – *cure* of disease, moral, mental and physical, and *education* in self-control and self-dependence. The community may well say to any of its members, "If you cannot support yourself by your own work, it is a pity. We will support you by our work, but we will not make it so pleasant for you that you will desire to continue the condition, and we will train your mind and body so that you will be able soon to undertake the care of yourself . . ."[57]

The AICP

The AICP tried to keep alive its belief that moral elevation was more important than the relieving of physical want, but it was, in fact, a losing battle. Physical needs were too insistent. In a set of confidential instructions to the visitors of the AICP the principles of the society are put forward as, "*First* the moral and physical elevation of the poor; and *Second,* . . . the relief of their necessities."[58] But it is reported that "this order, unhappily, has too often been reversed." The author, probably R. M. Hartley, who may have been the first person to make a career in America of administering a social agency, makes the rather startling admission that moral elevation is not what the poor themselves would prefer. "The poor seek relief, not reform; they ask bread, not counsel." But the well-to-do knew better. "It is worse to debase by alms than to withhold them; physical needs must be subservient to the moral" and present need be ignored in favor of "permanent elevation."[59]

The solution of this problem was to "aid those whom (the Society) can physically and morally elevate, and no others." Those whom the Society could not morally and physically elevate should be referred to the Almshouse, which "is a *legal* charity. It has no choice of subjects. It is bound to relieve all not otherwise legally provided for, without regard to character, for the obvious reason, if neglected by it, they might perish."[60]

The Salvation Army

One movement which denied both of these principles did occur, however, some years later. This was the work of William Booth and the Salvation Army. Although Booth's overwhelming purpose was evangelism, he had the sense to see that physical needs might have to be met first. He was also ready to work with what looked to the world the most hopeless cases. Unlike the moral reformers from the mainline denominations who were becoming increasingly secular in their thinking, he saw sin not as a failure to live up to accepted norms of industry, thrift, and sexual morality but as a common human condition due to the absence of God in one's life. He was therefore willing to meet it wherever it was found.

Charles Loring Brace

William Booth may not, however, have been the first to see the importance of meeting physical needs first. Charles Loring Brace, who is chiefly known for his work in resettling vagrant and homeless children in foster homes in the Midwest, reports a "new and practical movement of religious reform" that had passed over Europe in the years 1848-1853. He described it as the "entire breaking away from the old methods of religious influence, and *adapting themselves to the practical wants of these* (the poor)." He makes a curious equation between meeting physical needs and changing a person's whole environment and notes religious opposition to it:

> To give a poor man bread before a tract . . . to urge the entire change of circumstances and the emigration to country homes, as of far more importance to a certain class of vagrant children than any possible influence of Sunday-Schools or Chapel, to talk of cleanliness as the first steps to godliness – all this seemed then to have a "humanitarian" tendency, and to belong to European "socialism" and "infidelity."[61]

He himself admitted that although it was "right that those who loved humanity in its lowest forms should labor for the forlorn prostitute, and the mature criminal . . . no lasting effects could be expected to society from such efforts."[62] He therefore turned to children as being much more hopeful subjects.

There was still, however, the desire to take over control. As a District Conference of the Charity Organization movement in 1883 reports:

We have had our failures. We have not succeeded in reforming the lazy people in our charge, nor in rescuing their children, because the parents will not allow their children to go from home. Several times, we could have put them in good homes, if the parents had consented . . .[63]

The assumption here that these people were "in our charge" and that they were somehow at fault for not allowing their children to be placed in "good homes" argues a lack of understanding that is almost monumental. It explains why the next stage in trying to meet the problems of poverty, the Charity Organization Society, was lampooned as:

Organized charity, measured, and iced, in the name of a cautious, statistical Christ.[64]

Charity Organization

Investigate

As social conditions for the poor worsened under the impact of the Industrial Revolution and America also had to contend with a vast influx of immigrants, social reformers turned to Charity Organization. In many ways this was a continuation of what the Association for Improving the Condition of the Poor (AICP) had done. There was the same distaste for giving relief and belief in the influence of the friendly visitor. As time went on, however, more and more relief had to be given and Verl Lewis calculates that only one family in seven had a friendly visitor assigned to them. More and more the real work of the Society was carried out by paid agents who investigated families and granted emergency relief.[65]

The "fundamental law" of the Charity Organization Society (COS), according to one of its early leaders, was "expressed in one word, INVESTIGATE. Its motto is: 'No relief (except in the extreme cases of despair or imminent death) without previous and searching examination.'"[66] Indeed, the detection of fraud, which is described as the Society's *repressive* work, is listed as the Society's first function, ahead of the adequate relief of the honest poor and the reclaiming of the pauperized poor (its *benevolent* work), the establishment of "various well-proved" schemes for the encouragement of thrift and self-help (its *provident* work) and the suppression of social abuses (its *reformatory* work).[67]

It saw as the principal cause of pauperism the "misdirected charity of benevolent people" and believed this to have dragged the poor "to the lowest depths of confirmed pauperism," in which, "if left to themselves . . . they will inevitably sink lower and lower, till perchance they end their course in suicide or felony." [68]

It had, in fact, some difficulty in relating what it was doing to Christian charity. One writer analyzes the motives of many Christians as "subterfuges used by indolence and self-love when these would masquerade as charity" (probably not too inaccurate a description), but insists that "within its sphere of human life, the principles of Organized Charity are the truth."[69] Another does a very clever piece of theologizing in which he argues that there must be a "law of love" which must give rise to a system, and therefore become a science, which he calls the "science of social therapeutics".[70]

The Science of Social Therapeutics

The fact that the actual judgments made, on the basis of the most careful examination, were often moral ones and hardly scientific at all, is not addressed, but it seems to argue that the value-system inherent in the society of that time was assumed to be both scientifically and providentially ordained. Verl Lewis says that:

> Both laissez-faire economics and the evolutionary social theory of Herbert Spencer and William Graham Sumner were the underlying assumptions of charity organizations. As theists, COS leaders viewed prevailing social arrangements as manifestations of divine intent.[71]

He believes that this ideological system began to crumble before the pressures of professionalism and the impact of the Progressive movement with its emphasis on individual personality. He adds that "*Noblesse oblige* had largely submerged the ties of Nineteenth-Century humanitarianism to the egalitarian assumptions of the Quakers and Unitarians."[72]

But although *noblesse oblige* was certainly part of the problem and was obviously struggling with self-fulfillment, and while judgmentalism, despite assertions to the contrary, was still very much present, the particular flavor of the movement was the belief that it now had a science by which it could solve the problem, and this neither professionalism nor the Progressive movement could alter. The Charity Organization leaders may have been theists; they were certainly Modern Gnostics and their religion was Humanist-Positivist-Utopian.

There is one probably facetious statement in the writing of that time arguing against the classification of the poor as "worthy" or "unworthy." The author asks whether "any man can be unworthy of real help from other men?" and believes "obtrusive responsibility and piety" serve "as stock in trade for chronic helplessness and voluntary pauperism." However, his definition of "real help" includes "not infrequently, the sound application of a cat-o-nine tails."[73] The whole image is in fact of a discipline imposed on the poor rather than any understanding of what the poor themselves aspired to. One cannot help but sympathize with the British writer who longed for "some outpouring of comfortable, unhesitating, old-fashioned joyous bounty . . . if only it might be innocently indulged in."[74]

Efforts at Reform

In the United States

There were, in the Nineteenth Century, several people who gave their lives to some cause of benefit to the poor. In the United States one might mention John Augustus, a shoemaker, who was the first unofficial probation officer, Thomas Eddy, in prison reform, Dorothea Dix in her campaign for the humane treatment of the insane, Joseph Lee, with his interest in playgrounds, Clara Barton, who founded the American Red Cross, and Jacob Riis who was concerned with tenement housing.

In addition, a number of people concerned with the Charity Organization Society or similar organizations became instruments of reform or instituted programs for the poor not having to do with relief. Zebulon Brockway was active in prison reform, Robert De Forest in the problem of tenements, Homer Folks in public health, Charles Loring Brace in the placement of homeless children, and Edward T. Devine in the control and prevention of tuberculosis. There was some realization that external as well as internal conditions needed to be corrected. There was concern in some quarters about the way that the poor were treated in almshouses and hospitals. We have already noted the reforming efforts of the Settlement workers and in particular Jane Addams' advocacy for labor unions.

In England

In England, perhaps more than in the United States, it was possible for the well-to-do to espouse Socialist doctrines, as did, for instance,

Daisy, countess of Warwick, and shortly after the turn of the Century, Winston S. Churchill, or so it was held at the time. Indeed, liberal British writing at that time begins to show a new concern for social justice. Samuel Barnett, a British reformer, says, for instance:

> Generally it is assumed that the chief change is that to be effected in the habits of the poor. All sorts of missions and societies exist for the working of this change. Perhaps it is more to the purpose that a change be effected in the habits of the rich. Society has settled itself on a system which it never questions. It is assumed to be absolutely within a man's right to live where he chooses and to get the most for his money. It is this practice of living in pleasant places which impoverishes the poor.[75]

He attributes to absentee landlordism many of the problems that the poor encounter, including their physical debility and their resentment of the rich, and adds, "The fault did not begin with the poor; the rich sin, but the poor, made poorer and more angry, suffer the most."[76] On the other hand, it is also interesting to find a writer deploring what he calls the "mistaken and perverse" actions of the poor in refusing work at "the reduced rate of wages which was all their impoverished employers could afford to offer them" but asserting that they had "an irrefutable claim" to be idle, rather than to work except on their own terms, "however foolish or short-sighted they may have been to exercise" this claim.[77] Henry George, in what might be called a secular restatement of Ambrose's belief that personal property was the result of the Fall, contends that nature intended man to live on and use land:

> Is there not, therefore, a violation of the intent of nature in human laws which give to one more land than he can possibly use, and deny any land to the other?[78]

Although a number of the reformers were so because of religious conviction, there was a memory at least of Rousseau's "man is born free but everywhere he is in chains." There was also no small infusion from Marx and Engels. It is therefore interesting to find a Socialist such as Beatrice Webb expressing the problem in terms of sin. Mrs. Webb wrote of a "new ferment" in Britain, which, she says, "is to be discovered in a new consciousness of sin among men of intellect and of property. This consciousness of sin," she went on:

. . . was a collective or class consciousness, amounting to conviction, that the industrial organization which had yielded rent, interest and profits on a stupendous scale, had failed to provide a decent livelihood and tolerable conditions for the majority of the inhabitants of Great Britain.[79]

The Medical Model

Individual Responsibility and Technology

It was left to America, with its tradition of individual responsibility and its belief in technology, to carry the scientific claims of Charity Organization almost to their logical conclusion and develop a new science, that of social casework.

Social work theory, at this point, becomes important to society's treatment of the poor. Although major policies were established in Washington, often in response to pressure groups or to public opinion or in the light of current ideology, it was social workers who were in actual contact with the poor and to a great extent determined how they were treated. And once social workers became professionals, they acted with somewhat greater autonomy, or perhaps less representatively, than did the volunteer who was herself closely identified with upper or middle class culture.

Mary Richmond and "Scientific Investigation"

The person most responsible for establishing a social work method and ethic, and developing this new "science," was Mary E. Richmond. She had been a Charity Organization worker; in fact, her first book was entitled *Friendly Visiting Among the Poor*.[80] Miss Richmond greatly enlarged and, it should be said, enhanced the art of investigation. Early in her career she wrote that:

> honest investigation means a sincere unbiased searching for the whole truth, including not merely the dry facts, but that setting of circumstances and opportunity in which the facts exist.[81]

She was extremely rigorous in determining her data; the subchapter in her major work, *Social Diagnosis*, in which she compares social and legal evidence, is beautifully reasoned and does ensure the greatest possible objectivity. But the "whole" truth she sets out to find is what she calls "the wider self" or "the whole man" and is a mechanistic concept. "The mind of man," she writes, "(and in a very real sense the mind *is* the man) can be described as the sum of his social relationships."[82]

Her method was the answering of literally hundreds of questions about the individual and his or her relationships. For instance, she asks as one of the forty-six items about an unmarried mother:

> 15. When did girl's sexual experience begin? Under what circumstances – was it with a relative, an employer, an older man, a school boy? Has she accepted money from any man or men for unchastity, or has she received only a good time – theaters, dinner, etc. – or board? Has she lived for any period of time as the wife of any man or men. Has she supplemented her income through men or made her whole livelihood in this way? If so, for how long and when? Has she been a common prostitute, has she had a succession of "friends," or has she been intimate with only the one man? Has she a court record? From what she, her relatives, friends and employers say, does she seem to seek wrongdoing, or does she merely yield when evil approaches her?[83]

Two things might be said at this point. One is that with twenty or more times this information one might have a vast knowledge of the girl's behavior but the judgments that have to be made on it are not specified, and indeed still seem to remain largely in the moral sphere. There is a distinct element of assigning blame. These judgments are scarcely scientific, although they may be common sense; i.e., if the girl seeks wrongdoing one might try to restrain her, but if she yields to temptation protect her in some way. It might, however, be hard to distinguish between the two. And the other thing is, how does one help her?

Treatment

There is, in fact, a wealth of diagnosis but very little said about treatment. For the most part this consisted in environmental manipulation, but there was also some continued reliance on influence, persuasion, and exhortation to follow the course of action prescribed by the visitor. There was also a new element, not learned from any social science, but from practice. One would expect, after so detailed and so comprehensive a diagnosis, a very careful prescription. But what Mary Richmond actually described as the "most successful casework policies" were a curious trio: "encouragement and stimulation, the fullest possible participation of the client in all plans, and the skillful use of repetition."[84]

Client Self-Determination

It is the second of these that is significant. For the first time, the poor or deviant person being studied was given some part in his or her own treatment. In a later book, Miss Richmond elaborated on this principle and gave it the name by which it is still known: "self-determination."[85] However, she saw it not as a right, but as a pragmatic way of helping people; they did better if one allowed them to arrive, as much as possible, at plans for themselves rather than simply being prescribed for by others. Miss Richmond called it "one of the foundations stones of casework," but it was, at first, more of a piece of practice wisdom than a guiding principle, judging by some of the casework practiced at that time.

Miss Richmond also described casework as "the art of doing different things for and with different people by cooperating with them to achieve at one and the same time their own and society's betterment."[86] This does put the emphasis on the worker cooperating with the client, as those being treated were now to be known, rather than the client with the worker. However, it is, perhaps, a rather optimistic assumption that an individual's and society's interests are the same. Those who were struggling with the rise of socialism in Europe might not have agreed. In the same book she describes casework as "those processes which develop personality through adjustments, consciously effected, individual by individual, between men and their social environment."[87]

Social Casework and Professionalism

Social casework, now written as two words instead of three, as a discipline and a method, arose out of the Charity Organization Societies and represents the professionalization, in the name of science, of work with the poor and the distressed. Charity Organization had replaced undisciplined charity as a means of supporting the poor; now amateur friendly visiting was gradually eliminated by the employment of professionals.

The next step was obvious — the training of professionals — and in 1897 Miss Richmond herself made the first plea for a School of Applied Philanthropy. It is interesting, though, that in her plea she emphasizes not the need for greater scientific knowledge, but "better habits of thought and higher ideals" as the benefits to be gained.[88] She does not specify in what way the ideals of the untrained worker need to be elevated.

81

Social casework is an entirely American invention. There might be some speculation as to why this was so. It developed at a time when the order of things in Europe was being threatened with real or potential revolution. The social reformers of America believed neither in the class war nor in the kind of Tory socialism of which Barbara Tuchman accuses Beatrice and Sydney Webb:

> Coldly bent on improving society, they were essentially authoritarian, impatient with the democratic process . . . What was needed was a strong party with no nonsense and a businesslike understanding of national needs which would take hold of the future like a governess, slap it into clean clothes, wash its face, blow its nose, make it sit up straight at table and eat a proper diet.[89]

Rather, it saw the solution to the problem of poverty to be the adjustment of individuals to the prevailing culture.

It rarely questioned this culture. There were injustices that needed to be remedied, but the culture as a whole was beneficent. There was no overweening "Social Problem" such as even the British recognized and no real Labour Party in Congress, as there was at Westminster as early as 1906. The nearest America came to it was Eugene Debs' 900,000 votes in 1912, and the nearest to revolution the Pullman Strike and Coxey's Army. There was no entrenched aristocracy to overthrow and enough upward mobility possible that America thought not so much in terms of a class or a system as of a personal failure to adjust. While European countries were attempting to deal with poverty by means of social insurance and child labor statutes, American social work, despite the reforming efforts of Jane Addams, the Abbott sisters, Julia Lathrop, and others, became more and more identified with the treatment of the individual, largely on a medical model. Social casework and social work became almost synonymous.

Notes

The Humanist-Positivist-Utopian Belief

[1] James Leiby, "Social Welfare: History of Basic Ideas," *Enclyclopedia of Social Work*, Seventeenth Edition, Washington, D. C., 1977. Volume II, p. 1516.

[2] Ibid., p. 1517, quoting Amos Warner, *American Charities*, 1894.

[3] Ibid., p. 1517.

[4] Ibid.

[5] Reinold Niebuhr, *The Contribution of Religion to Social Work*, New York, 1932, pp. 32-33. One might point out also that although Darwin was thought "godless," Spencer and Sumner were believed by many religious people. See Smylie, "Gilder, Gilt and the Needle's Eye," p. 5.

[6] Herbert Bisno, *The Philosophy of Social Work*, Washington, D. C., 1952, p.6.

[7] Ibid., p. 6.

[8] Halmos, *The Faith of the Counselors*, pp. 74ff.

[9] See D. W. Harding's review of Philip Reiff's *Freud: The Mind of a Moralist* in the *Spectator* (1960), February 12:226 and Gisela Knopka's *Eduard C. Lindeman and Social Work Philosophy*, Minneapolis, 1958, p. 185.

[10] The one most amusing exception is Samuel Butler's *Erewhon*, published in 1872, which is a satire on the society of the time in the form of an Utopia.

[11] The theme of maximizing one's potential is very obvious in most modern social work literature. The first three values of social work, according to Father F. P. Biestek, depending on a belief in the dignity and worth of man, are that man has potentiality, a thrust towards realization, and a right to appropriate means of realizing it, "Problems in Identifying Social Work Values," in *Values in Social Work: a Re-examination*, #9 in a Series of Regional Institutes offered by the National Association of Social Workers, New York, 1964, p. 24.

[12] The fulfillment of "needs" is basic to nearly all social work literature. It is perhaps best exemplified by Charlotte Towle's well-known book, *Common Human Needs*, Washington, D. C., 1945, which was sponsored by the United States Government but later withdrawn because of an ambiguous statement about "socialization" which the American Medical Association took to be recommending "socialized medicine."

[13] Gordon Hamilton, "The Underlying Philosophy of Social Casework," in Cora Kasius, editor, *Principles and Techniques in Social Case Work: Selected Articles*, 1940-1950, New York, 1950, p. 10.

[14] Robert Waelder, "The Scientific Approach to Casework with Special Emphasis on Psychoanalysis," in Kasius, *Principles and Techniques*, pp. 24-25.

[15] Bisno, *The Philosophy of Social Work*, pp .25-26. Bisno is particularly critical of Catholic social work, probably because Catholic social work has been much more explicit about its philosophy than have Protestants, and CP's who are largely Protestant and are not much interested in social work except to condemn it.

[16] F. R. Barry, *The Relevance of Christianity*, London, 1931, pp .111-112.

[17] "Nakas' to Skobeliev," reprinted in John Reed, *Ten Days that Shook the World*, England, 1926, p. 270.

[18] A. V. Lunatcharsky, "On Popular Education," Decree of the Council of People's Commissars, 1917, reproduced in Reed (ibid.), p. 298.

[19] F. P. Biestek calls this the supreme value in the hierarchy of social work values ("Problems in Identifying Social Work Values," p. 23). Bisno calls it "the most fundamental premise of all" and emphasizes that man earns it "by the very fact of his existence." *The Philosophy of Social Work*, p. 5.

[20] See A. P. Miles, *American Social Work Theory: A Critique and Proposal*, New York, 1954, p. 22.

[21] Barry, *Relevance of Christianity*, p. 122.

[22] Berdyaev, *Slavery and Freedom*, p. 44.

The Settlement Movement

[23] See Chapter 1, note 19.

[24] Samuel A. Barnett, "Distress in East London," an article in *The Nineteenth Century* (now the *Nineteenth Century and After*, November 1886, reproduced in Michael Goodwin, editor, *Nineteenth Century Opinion*, London, 1951, p. 65.

[25] There is a good description of the beginning of a settlement in a book by Mrs. H. F. Freeman, *Lend a Hand*, 1890, excerpted by Ralph E. and Muriel W. Pumphrey, *The Heritage of American Social Work*, New York and London, 1961, pp. 197-201.

[26] Jane Addams, "The Subjective Necessity for Social Settlements," in Jane Addams et al., *Philanthropy and Social Progress*, New York, 1893, pp. 1-26.

[27] Allen F. Davis, "Settlements: History," in the *Encyclopedia of Social Work*, 17th Issue, 1977, p. 1270.

[28] Robert A. Woods, "University Settlements as Laboratories of Social Science," 1893, reproduced by Pumphrey and Pumphrey, *The Heritage*, p. 208.

[29] John P. Gavit, reported by Mary E. Richmond, in a letter 1899, reproduced by Pumphrey and Pumphrey, *The Heritage*, p. 262. There is a most interesting satire on middle–class mission to the poor in Samuel Butler's, *The Way of All Flesh*, published in 1903 but written about 1884. In one episode Ernest, the young preacher, is shocked by his friend's reaction to his question, "Don't you like poor people very much yourself?" and comes to understand that "no one was nice for being poor, and that between the upper and lower classes there was a gulf which amounted practically to an impassable barrier." Everyman Edition, p. 281.

[30] Jane Addams, "The Subtle Problems of Charity," 1899, excerpted by Pumphrey and Pumphrey, *The Heritage*, p. 275.

[31] Ibid.

[32] John H. Griscom, M. D., *The Sanitary Condition of the Laboring Population of New York*, New York, 1845, excerpted ibid., pp. 96-102.

[33] Robert Treat Paine, "Pauperism in Great Cities: Its Four Chief Causes," 1893, reproduced ibid., pp. 230-231.

[34] Amos G. Warner, "Notes on the Statistical Determination of the Causes of Poverty," 1889, reproduced ibid., p. 241. It is curious to see, among the "habits producing and produced by the subjective characteristics," the moralistic ones of "lubricity" and "sexual self-abuse."

[35] Amos G. Warner, "The Causes of Poverty Further Considered," 1894, reproduced ibid., pp. 248-249. Warner comments on the low incidence of "misconduct" and high amount of sickness among "colored" people. He also thinks that they did not come to the attention of relief agencies because of their fear of them. He does not remark on the high incidence of drunkenness his statistics show among the Irish.

[36] Davis, "Settlements: History," p. 1268.

[37] Ibid., pp. 1269,1270

[38] Allen F. Davis, *Spearheads for Reform the Social Settlements and the Progressive Movement, 1890-1914*, New York, 1967, pp. 34-35.

Paternalism

[39] In North Carolina, for instance, the "juvenile judge" in many counties was the Clerk of Court, a position which did not require legal training as late as the 1960s.

[40] Roscoe Pound, foreword in Pauline V. Young, *Social Treatment in Probation and Delinquency*, New York, 1952.

[41] *Commonwealth vs. Fisher,* 213 Pa. 48, 62 Atl. 198, 200.

[42] See, for instance, Herbert H. Lou, *Juvenile Courts in the United States,* Chapel Hill, N. C., 1927.

[43] Ibid., p. 2.

[44] Judge Marion Woodward, in a letter published in the Social Service Review, 18 (1944):368.

[45] Roscoe Pound, quoted in U. S. Department of Health, Education and Welfare, *Standard for Juvenile and Family Courts,* Washington, D. C., 1966, p. 3.

[46] Jane Addams, "The Subtle Problems," reproduced by Pumphrey and Pumphrey, *The Heritage*, p. 274.

[47] Ibid., p.275.

[48] R. E. Thompson, *Manual for Visitors Among the Poor,* Philadelphia, 1879, reproduced ibid., p. 177.

[49] Quoted by Davis, "Settlements: History," p. 1268.

[50] Miss H. F. Freeman, in *Lend a Hand*, exerpted by Pumphrey and Pumphrey, *The Heritage*, p. 200.

The "Christian Socialists" and the Friendly Visitors

[51] Thompson, *Manual for Visitors*, pp. 176-181.

[52] Ibid., P. 180.

[53] Ibid., p. 177.

[54] Quoted by de Schweinitz, *England's Road*, p .145.

[55] Evidence before the Royal Commission on the Aged Poor, 1895, reproduced by Lubbock, *Some Relief Questions*, p. 275.

[56] Josephine Shaw Lowell, "The Economic and Moral Effects of Public Outdoor Relief," 1890, reproduced by Pumphrey and Pumphrey, *The Heritage*, p. 225.

[57] Ibid., p. 224.

[58] "Confidential Instructions to the Visitors of the AICP," December 1855, reproduced by Pumphrey and Pumphrey, *The Heritage,* p .110.

[59] Ibid.

[60] Ibid.

[61] Charles Loring Brace, "Short Sermons to News Boys," New York, 1866, reproduced by Pumphrey and Pumphrey, *The Heritage,* p .115-116.

[62] Ibid., p. 115.

[63] *Fourth Annual Report of the Associated Charities of Boston,* 1883, reproduced by Pumphrey and Pumphrey, *The Heritage,* p. 181.

[64] Quoted in this instance from Elmer Rice's play *Street Scene,* 1929, where it is written in dialect.

Charity Organization

[65] Verl Lewis, "Charity Organization Society," *Encyclopedia of Social Work,* 1977 Edition, pp. 98-99.

[66] Rev. S. Humphreys Gurteen, *A Handbook of Charity Organization,* Buffalo, 1882, reproduced by Pumphrey and Pumphrey, *The Heritage* p. 170.

[67] Ibid., p. 172.

[68] Ibid., pp .170-171.

[69] Charles J. Bonaparte, "The Ethics of Organized Charity, 1893, reproduced by Pumphrey and Pumphrey, *The Heritage,* p. 191.

[70] Rev. D. O. Kellogg, "The Principle and Advantage of Association in Charities," 1880, reproduced, ibid., pp. 174-175.

[71] Lewis, "Charity Organization . . ," p. 100.

[72] Ibid.

[73] Bonaparte, "The Ethics of Organized Charity," p. 184.

[74] Caroline Emilia Stephan, "Receiving Strangers," 1879, reprinted in Michael Goodwin, Ed., *Nineteenth Century Opinion* p. 71.

Efforts at Reform

[75] Samuel A. Barnett, "Distress in East London," 1886, reprinted in Goodwin, *Nineteenth Century Opinion,* p .67.

[76] Ibid., p. 66.

[77] W. R. Greg, " Grave Perplexity Before Us," 1879, reproduced, ibid., pp .68-69.

[78] Henry George, "The Reduction to Iniquity," 1884, reproduced, ibid., p. 63.

[79] Beatrice Webb, *My Apprenticeship,* London, 1926, quoted by de Schweinitz , *England's Road,* p. 1166.

The Medical Model

[80] New York, 1899.

[81] "What is Charity Organization?" *Charities Review*, 9 (January 1900), quoted in Lewis, "Charity Organization," p. 99.

[82] Mary Richmond, *Social Diagnosis*, New York, 1917, p. 368.

[83] Ibid., p. 416.

[84] Mary Richmond, *What is Social Case Work?*, New York, 1922, p. 256.

[85] Ibid.

[86] Mary Richmond, "The Social Case Worker in a Changing World," 1915, reprinted in *The Long View*, a collection of her articles published posthumously, New York, 1930, pp. 374-375.

[87] Ibid.

[88] Mary Richmond, "The Need for a Training School in Applied Philanthropy," 1897, reproduced in Pumphrey and Pumphrey, *The Heritage*, p. 291.

[89] Barbara Tuchman, *The Proud Tower*, New York, 1966, Bantam Books Edition, p. 420.

CHAPTER 4

Toward Entitlement: Freud, the Depression, and the New Deal

The Impact of Freud

A New Profession in Search of a Legitimized Theory

The new profession of social work, in itself an American invention, was ready for Freud, or at least the early, optimistic Freud, when his work became known in America in the 1920s. Here was an acceptably scientific theory that explained much of what had puzzled caseworkers when clients had not responded to reason. And in as far as social workers had developed, as many had, empathy for their clients, here was an answer to capitalist-puritan moralism which, in any case, was out of fashion after the first World War. The Depression at the end of the decade only made Freud's theories more acceptable. People were obviously not responsible for their poverty – why, tomorrow, I might be out of a job. There was a sense of common human vulnerability to forces, both external and internal. It produced for a time, at a personal level, the most empathic and humane treatment of those in trouble the country had ever known, despite the inadequacy of relief and the rigors of the Depression.

The Freudian Model

It was not so much Freud's actual findings, which have been subject to many revisions, which changed American social work. It was his utterly new way of looking at people in trouble. There were, in the main, four elements in this:

1. The emphasis on biological and experiential determinism – that is, that people will behave in accordance with their biological inheritance and their early childhood experiences, no matter how unreasonable this behavior may seem.
2. The assertion of the common vulnerability of humanity. Psychosis and neurosis are not illnesses that strike some and not others. We are all a little neurotic, but some of us more so than others. As Norman O. Brown has pointed out, this is the psychoanalytic analogue of the theological doctrine of original sin.[1]

3. The practice of looking at the world through the eyes of the client – what he is thinking or feeling about it – rather than looking at him as the world sees him, from the outside. There is a close analogy here with Buber's distinction between "I-Thou" and "I-It" relationships.[2]
4. The importance of relationship in the therapeutic process.

Philosophy Rather than Science

Freud's impact at first was much more that of a philosopher than a scientist. His philosophic teaching was in fact in keeping with the liberal thought of the time, but curiously enough it was justified as science. Thus, Philip Klein ascribes the new way of looking at people from the inside out, as it were, to social work's "new scientific character" which shifted its perspective

> from an external view previously held by social reformers, theorists and philanthropists alike, in which the poor, the sick, the criminal or the neglected child appeared mainly in contrast to the normal and quantitatively solid mass of population, to an analytic view as from the angle of the client himself. The social worker in this new conception was no longer an agent serving the social mechanism as much as an instrument of adjustment manipulated in the interest of the client and upon the physical and social environment of the client.[3]

The shift is, however, a philosophical or even a political one, rather than the result of new scientific knowledge. Science was also credited with dispelling

> a belief that under ordinary conditions people are in need through some fault of their own, a belief rooted in our culture, fostered by religious injunctions, nourished by education and verified by the success magazines, a belief that could be routed by the most elementary understanding of the economics of an industrial society,as modern psychology has replaced the belief in witchcraft. . .[4]

It is even given the credit for discovering that starvation and embarrassment are not effective social stimuli. "Making life more miserable for the mothers and children," says one writer, "by starvation, punishment and embarrassment are methods that are unscientific."[5] They are, of course, also inhumane.

How pervasive this belief in science as the answer to all problems was, is shown by Gordon Hamilton, in her attack on the "Functional" school of social work (the differences of which from the prevailing "Organismic" or "Diagnostic" School were more philosophical than scientific, despite their adherence to different psychoanalytic models). "I must also remind you," she said, "that we can only have schools of thought *before* conclusive scientific data are secured."[6]

Klein, however, who despite his apparent rejection of a social norm in the passage quoted above, believed that social work is

> specifically oriented towards deliberately changing the conditions of individuals from what was found socially undesirable to what is socially acceptable

and adds

> the decision as to what shall be socially desirable or undesirable is a function of community mores and is, therefore, an a priori postulate not subject to scientific verification.[7]

So, it might be remarked, is the way in which people should be treated and the freedom that they should have to manage their own lives.

Uses of the New "Knowledge"

There were, in fact, two ways in which the new knowledge could be used. In its broad philosophical aspects it could only lead to greater freedom for the individual and this could be shown to be "scientific." But once something is given this label it infers knowledge which only the expert can have and this immediately puts power into the hands of the expert.

Virginia Robinson, whose book did most to introduce social work to analytical thinking, foresaw the problem. The new knowledge, she said, could be used to create "relationship as a new environment which gives the client opportunity to work out his own problems," or it could result in a "point to point relationship in which the worker manipulates the client's inner life as before she manipulated the environment."[8] It was on this matter that the "diagnostic" and the "functional" schools fundamentally differed.

The Principle of Self-Determination

Moral Principle or Utilitarian Practice Principles

The first impact of the new knowledge was to give scientific authority to what was basically a philosophical principle. Mary Richmond, as we have seen, had enunciated a pragmatic principle that she called self-determination. Freud's biological determinism gave this scientific sanction. In a classic statement, Bertha Reynolds wrote:

> If we accept the foregoing as a true, though necessarily inadequate, picture of the illumination which began to trickle into social case work through its contact with dynamic psychiatry, the futility of coercion becomes increasingly evident. It is no longer a question of whether it is *wrong* to try to make our fellow beings think and feel as we want them to. In the long run it is simply silly. The vital needs of their being will in the end determine what they shall feel and how they shall act.[9]

But it is also wrong, and wholly contrary to the philosophy of this new profession.

Miss Reynolds herself was a radical who worked for the National Maritime Union. Many young social workers were avowed socialists or communists. Self-determination, which had begun as a pragmatic tool, had now seemingly been confirmed by science (it is curious that Freud's determinism was the first of his principles to be abandoned later).[10] Finally, it became recognized as a philosophical and even a religious belief.

It was formulated as a right which the social worker granted to his clients. Swithun Bowers, a Catholic priest who contributed much to social work theory, wrote: "We must not and cannot take away this fundamental freedom, given to man by God, to choose the means for the attainment of his personal destiny."[11]

Secular writers tended to see the pragmatic value of self-determination but also recognized its moral implications. Miss Hamilton italicizes the principle: "Help is more effective if the recipient participates actively and responsibly in the process," but adds, "This is certainly a basic democratic concept."[12] Florence Hollis calls client-self-determination "the most widely held principle in the field of casework" and says that the multiple objective of casework is more likely to be achieved "if the caseworker recognizes that the client must be in control of the guiding of his own life — making for himself the choices that are necessary to fitting his own desires into the social fabric."[13]

The principle also acquired a fourth meaning. It became an ideal to which social workers were urged to produce in their clients and to "maximize" self-determination became a social work goal.[14]

Consequences

Self-determination as a principle certainly produced a much more humane treatment of the poor. At times it may have led to indulgence, to protecting people from the law or the natural consequences of their actions. There was a tendency, in Freudian terms, to liberate the id at the expense of the superego. But it did much to eliminate the disabilities which had been taken for granted as part of the fate of anyone who asked for help – submission to the will of the helper and restrictions on his freedom to manage his own life. As Miss Hamilton said, "Social workers do not impose upon the client their own goals and standards, their own solutions and morals."[15]

The Real Problem

Yet the very synthesis of a "fact," a practice method, a goal, and a political belief into a moral principle [16] obscured the real problem, which was not, "How much self-determination should people have?" but, "To what extent should being poor or in trouble and having to ask for help limit the self-determination that other people enjoy?"

The former, as Helen Harris Perlman has pointed out, is somewhat illusory.[17] Nevertheless, there have been a number of attempts to identify how much self-determination should be permitted, allowed, or granted. Hollis would permit it "until it is demonstrated that the exercise of this right would be highly detrimental to himself and others.[18] Father Biestek saw it as limited by the "client's capacity for positive and constructive self-determination," "limitations arising from agency function."[19] Saul Bernstein, while demoting self-determination from "king" to "citizen" among social work values, delineates six levels of self-determination, each more responsible than the last.[20]

But, except for the limitation imposed by law (and even then one may be free to break the law and accept the consequences), these limitations all suggest that the poor and the troubled are only free to manage their own affairs when they do so in a way that social workers consider to be constructive or, in Biestek's case, moral. They are still less free than the well-to-do. It took that clear thinker, Grace Marcus, however, to expose the basic fallacy in "granting" self-determination as a right. "How difficult it is," she wrote, at a time when the principle was in the forefront of all social work thinking,

> to accept this harsh truth, is revealed by our distortion of it into the facile concept of "self-determination," whereby we can relapse once more in a comforting dependence on free will and, by talking of self-determination as a "right," flatter ourselves that a fact which is often intolerably painful to the individual and to society is still within our power to concede or refuse as a social benefit.[21]

The principle is perhaps an example of a humanistic belief that had no real theological roots, despite Biestek's assertion that it derives from man's "obligation for self-realization" owed to his Creator.[22] It is too easy to modify, to reinterpret, to balance with other supposed goods, or to demote in importance.

A Check on Social Control

Nevertheless, it was, at least in its early manifestation, of enormous use. It was a great corrective to pride arising out of exercising social control. That came, ironically, from its deterministic base. As Lionel Trilling has said, biological determinism

> is actually a liberating idea . . . It suggests that there is a residue of human quality beyond the reach of cultural control, and that this residue of human quality, elemental as it may be, serves to bring culture itself under criticism and keeps it from being absolute.[23]

It forbade to social workers many former practices. Biestek, despite the limitations on the principle he had promulgated, produced a very useful list of allowable and unallowable actions. It is permissible to help the client see his problems more clearly, to acquaint him with resources in the community, to "introduce stimuli that will activate the client's dormant resources," and to "create a relationship in which the client can grow and work out his own problems." It is impermissible to assume the principal responsibility for the working out of the problem; to insist on a minute scrutiny of the social or emotional life of the client, regardless of the service he requests; to determine the treatment plan and superimpose it on the client; to manipulate, directly or indirectly, the social or emotional life of the client; to persuade, to control or direct and to advise and offer plans in such a way that the client feels forced to accept the caseworker's suggestions.[24]

Unfortunately, today doing nearly all of these things is common and accepted practice. However, in a recent article (advocating what amounts to deceptive techniques to get clients to do what the social worker wants), the principle of self-determination is quoted to suggest that these practices be used on clients only when client and social worker have mutually agreed-on goals (but are not to be used on the public or public officials).[25]

Self-determination did more. In its political aspect it helped to develop a welfare system that established, for the first time, a legal right to assistance, and in its partnership with Freud's view from the inside out, it enabled a writer to say, with some justification,

> At its best, social casework can make the tenets of democratic living a deeply personal experience. Completely oriented to the individual and his very personal needs, it concentrates on him, trying to serve his purposes only, flexibly and in a non-directing way.[26]

Social Insurance and the Right to Assistance

The Promise of Dignity

While social workers were developing their theories of self-determination, the government in the United States was reacting to the Depression with a system that for the first time for more than a thousand years seemed to promise some dignity to the poor. What appeared to promise this was not, however, the social insurance features of the Social Security Act, but its humbler public assistance features.

The idea of social insurance had been around for a long time. "Friendly" societies had flourished in England in the Eighteenth Century. As early as 1768 an act of parliament had authorized a social insurance system for a whole county, but the scheme had foundered because of its voluntary nature.[27] A bill in 1788 had attempted to make the scheme compulsory and had even suggested forcing non-contributors to wear distinctive badges.[28] But so far from according the poor some status as contributors to their own welfare, when the idea of compulsory insurance was again mooted in 1878 the motive appeared to be to force the profligate and improvident poor to bear part of the cost of their support. As a writer at that time put it:

For it is a plain failure of good government that an enormous class of the people should be allowed to ignore the first duty of every loyal citizen, and it is a political crime of the gravest sort that they should be, as they are, encouraged in the notion that the greater their waste, their sensuality, their ignorance and their selfishness, the stronger claim they establish to support and aid from their fellow men.[29]

Europe, too, had long been familiar with social insurance. Bismarck had introduced a comprehensive plan in Germany in 1889; by 1903 eighteen million Germans were insured against accidents, thirteen millions against old age, and eleven million against illness.[30] This has generally been considered a measure taken not out of compassion for the poor, but as a concession to the Social Democrats to forestall labor strife. Much the same motives were ascribed to Lloyd George and Churchill in Britain twenty years later.

The Right to Assistance
What was really new in the American Social Security Act of 1935 were the categories of public assistance – at that time Old Age Assistance, Aid to the Needy Blind, and Aid to Dependent Children. These spelled out for the first time a legal and enforceable right to assistance provided certain eligibility conditions were met.

It is true that the law did not guarantee how great or even sufficient the grant should be. Less-eligibility could still be practiced. It is true that, especially in the Aid to Dependent Children program where grants had of necessity to be made to the caretakers of the children rather than to the children themselves, all sort of arguments have since been evinced to show that Congress did not mean this program to establish a right to assistance. One writer, for instance, took his stand on Congress having specified that the grant was being made "to or on behalf of children" despite the fact that the words "on behalf of" do not appear in the original act; the words in the act are "with respect to a dependent child."[31] Another believed that the unrestricted money payment was written into the program inadvertently because the legislators were thinking of old age assistance.[32] The Supreme Court of Missouri held that "Old age assistance benefits are not payments to which citizens are entitled to as a right," although what was involved in that case was a welfare director's right to deny assistance to an otherwise eligible man who chose to live a life dangerous to his health.[33]

But these arguments only go to show the resistance of those who could not accept the right of the poor to live their own lives free from efforts to reform or rehabilitate them. As Hollis and Taylor wrote:

> These ideas run counter to some of the most deeply ingrained traditional economic and welfare concepts of Western civilization. Many tenets of Christendom support the private enterprise system in the belief that economic aid provided by other than one's own endeavor or that of his family is by nature a gratuity that should be classified as charity rather than a right.[34]

Unrestricted Money Payments

Nevertheless, the "moral right" adumbrated by Ambrose and Aquinas had now been given statutory form, and was protected by a system of appeals or "fair hearings" in which due process was to be observed. That it was so was largely due to men such as Arthur J. Altmeyer, Karl de Schweinitz, and Delafield Smith.

De Schweinitz has described the process by which the simple words "money payments" were interpreted to mean unrestricted payments which the recipient could spend as he wished, free from social control, and which resulted in the following official statement:

> Assistance in the form of a money payment provides the recipient with a sum of money to be spend as he, not the agency, determines will best meet his need. It is made in recognition of the fact that a recipient of assistance does not, by reasons of financial dependence, lose his capacity to select how, when, and whether each of his requirements is to be met. It insures his right to use his payment with the same freedom as do persons who receive their income from other sources and to carry on his business through the normal channels of exchange.[35]

It is not, in fact, making a "money" payment. De Schweinitz ascribes this decision to the "basic principles of the law," and perhaps less convincingly, from the reports of congressional committees, from decisions of the courts, and from "prevalent political, economic, and social beliefs."[37]

The "Rights" Nature of the Programs

Arthur Altmeyer was equally positive about the "rights" nature of the programs:

> The Federal Social Security Act provides two kinds of programs -- public assistance and social insurance. In the one, rights are conditioned on need; in the other, on wage loss. Yet they are of the same kind, although people sometimes hold that those arising out of contributions paid by a person, or on his behalf, are the more valid. I do not believe that such a distinction can be made. We do not say that the right of parents to send a youngster to public school depends on whether or not they pay direct taxes.[38]

But the real philospher of the right to assistance was A. Delafield Smith, an assistant legal counsel of the Federal Security Agency. Smith held that the security provided by nature in the past was no longer available in an industrial society and that society must therefore create it artificially.

> It is not that society is becoming tender-hearted. The motivation is far more profound. It rests ultimately on the gradual assumption of functions formerly performed by nature.[39]

Within this society there must be no depressed class to which the general laws do not apply:

> The independence and unplanned, unregimented freedom of action of its rich and powerful members is not the test of a free society . . . (This is) found in the scope of right and privilege possessed by its weakest elements -- those who are under the greatest pressure to surrender their independence.[40]

People cannot really be independent until they can count on a predictable world ruled by law which would assure them of subsistence and other rights. This is an important insight. To be independent, persons need something on which they can depend. This may be class, as in Britain where the aristocracy are often the most independent thinkers, or wealth (we speak of people of "independent means"), or the love of

God, or the support of a family. Smith, who was essentially a humanist, put it this way:

> It is the fact of having a legal right to what we need, rather than the fact of having produced it or secured it by our own efforts, that furnishes the primary condition for preserving human dignity and independence. [41]

Moreover, this law is not conditioned by behavior:

> Law never seeks to buy behavior. It seeks to give rein to moral law. It seeks to allow the individual to benefit or suffer from his choices and sacrifices as freely as possible. This is quite inconsistent with the idea that behavior should enlarge or diminish legal rights.[42]

The Role of the Government

With the passage of the Social Security Act, the federal government became, in fact, the protector of the rights of the poor and of the least popular among them -- a role not unlike that of the medieval church. It intervened to prevent states from maintaining a waiting list in public assistance, a device whereby black applicants could, for instance, be effectually denied assistance by putting them lower on the list than their white neighbors. It took a stand against "suitable home" provisions in Aid to Dependent children.[43] It tried, less successfully, to prevent the publication of the names of welfare recipients.[44]

Control Fights Back

But the fact that it had to do so was ominous. "The prevalent political, economic and social beliefs," de Schweinitz had enunciated in the 1930s, were neither as prevalent as he believed, nor did they stand the test of time. The public found commutative justice hard to accept. Most of them still thought of assistance as a "dole" and were convinced that most of the recipients of public assistance were cheats.[45] As we have seen, responsible economists like Lewis Merriam thought that even those who received social security checks, to which they had contributed while working, should be subject to supervision. Less-eligibility was still rife in the system. The grants rarely, if ever, were sufficient for more than minimum health and decency, and many states paid only a fraction of their own estimate, often long outdated, of minimum needs. Despite the federal government's insistence that the client should be the principal source of information about his situation, as he is, for instance, in paying income tax, he was subjected to a degrading and often rigorous investigation, which almost assumed that he intended to lie or to cheat. Some states maintained "fraud squads" which would raid a recipient's house in the middle of the night to determine whether there was a man in the house, which would render a deserted mother ineligible.

But perhaps the greatest threat to the principle of the right to assistance came not from the public or the legislature but from the social work profession itself.

Responsibility and the Social Norm

The "Rights" Philosophy and Social Work Practice Theories

At first the social work profession, and particularly that branch of it which developed in Pennsylvania from the theories of Rank rather than Freud — the so-called "functional" school — accepted the "rights"philosophy wholeheartedly. In a classic statement Grace Marcus wrote:

> In administering assistance as a right, the agency is bound not to use the individual's economic helplessness for purposes that have not been generally declared and defined even though these purposes are presumably inspired by interest in the individual's welfare or the welfare of his dependents.[46]

Jane Hoey, who was chief of the Bureau of Public Assistance, carried the argument farther. She not only met head on the problem of those who might use money payments unwisely, which, she wrote:

> does not vitiate use of the principle for the great majority. Perhaps it does not vitiate it even for the unwise few when long range implications of other practices are considered.[47]

but she took a stand against well-meaning interference in clients' lives:

> When the agency discusses a problem of health with the family physician, or housing with the landlord, or of a child's behavior with the teacher, the intrusion into any one of these community relationships, even by the most skillful worker, may impair the normal function of the family.[48]

Ruth Smalley proclaimed a "new social casework" which clearly eschewed the ethic of social responsibility on the part of a superior class:

> the social worker makes no assumption that the person who comes to her is incapable of understanding or solving the problem, or that by virtue of having one problem he has many, or that if he has many, he must deal with them all in order to receive help with any. The old "social class" psychology out of which, however kindly, one person takes responsibility for another has gone out with the new social casework.[49]

But the predominant "organismic" or "diagnostic" school, despite its nominal adherence to the principle of self-determination, found itself frustrated. Unlike the "functional" school, which had declared that the social worker "with all his knowledge cannot determine – cannot even predict" the outcome of a case,[50] and had made clear, both on practical and on moral grounds, that it did not wish to do so, the diagnostic school did take responsibility for results, not only with those clients who sought its services, but those who did not.

"The theme of social responsibility," said one writer, "towards those who do not seek us out is being played louder and more surely as we pass the mid-century mark,[51] which was, in fact, about the time that this trend began to make itself apparent. It is true that she was writing about children, not necessarily on public assistance, but the diagnostic group as a whole had declared as one of its goals that it strove "to help the client achieve the approximation of a norm."[52]

Social Norms and Professional control

This norm was not, Gordon Hamilton insisted, "some norm of the caseworker's or agency's selection" as one critic, at least had held.[53] Rather it was a social norm dictated by the culture. Hamilton had herself laid the groundwork for such a theory when she quoted the anthropologist, Ruth Benedict, as saying:

> Just as those whose congenial responses are closest to that behavior which characterizes their society, so are those disoriented whose congenial responses fall into that arc of behavior which is not capitalized by their culture.[54]

101

This cultural norm was assumed to be entirely beneficial for the client. Adjustment to it was "a condition in which tensions may be relaxed and desires satisfied,"[55] in which the client may realize "his own capacity for change and growth,"[56] and achieve "the most productive life of which he is capable."[57] The fact remained that it was the social worker who interpreted the culture and its norm,and this was not very different from the efforts of the Christian Socialists and the Charity Organization Society to elevate the poor.

The right to represent the culture had, however, passed from those with social status to those who supposedly knew their social science. Indeed, one writer justifies intrusions into the lives of clients of social agencies, which would have been considered unethical a few years before, because "the current ethic of responsibility is set within a framework of knowledge and skills unknown to those who worked many years before us."[58] That those who were to be brought to approximate the norm included the poor is clear from Hamilton's statement that "we do not have the common sense to insist on rehabilitation as an inherent element in some categories of assistance." [59]

Attempted Reconciliation with Self-Determination

The fact that taking this kind of responsibility for other people made it hard to adhere to the principle of self-determination, was concealed even from those who believed in it by the use of two assumptions.

The first was that what was being offered was "services," which, even if people did not want them, they nonetheless needed. Hamilton held that "the right to assistance includes the right to receive social and psychological help."[60] At the same time, she maintained that "only diagnostic ability can insure that services are given *appropriately* as well as responsibly."[61] This would not seem to leave to the client much choice in the matter.

It is true that some poor people probably did want services and were either too suspicious or too proud to ask for them. Resistance to taking help is a well-known phenomenon in social work. Alice Overton wrote a very good article on serving families who could not verbalize their need for help,[62] but the methods she suggested did not depend on diagnosis as much as they did on a non-judgmental and empathic approach.

The second assumption was that, providing one's diagnosis was correct (and Lewis Lehrman was so sure of that, he wrote of the "truths" of diagnosis on which the worker could act "without fear,")[63] or one had gauged the culture correctly, then one was only doing what the client really wanted. Even Bertha Reynolds, whom we have seen as the staunchest believer that it is not only wrong but "simply silly" to try to make people think or feel as we want them to, concluded in her last book (although she was clearly worried about it) that diagnosis was not an imposition because it "is not imposing the thinking of a stranger with alien interests but weaving together the threads that both client and case worker draw from life and work on together.[64] Similarly, a worker from the United States Children's Bureau writes of neglectful parents:

> At first sight these facts may seem harsh in relation to the parent. But when these are made clear in an atmosphere that is warm, understanding and nonblaming by a child welfare worker who really wants to be helpful and believes in the parents' ability to improve their care of their children . . . they begin to feel that they, too, can become better parents and most parents want to be good parents. It is part of the total culture of the country.[65]

At the same time Herbert Bisno, who expresses the views of the diagnostic school in his *The Philosophy of Social Work*, was adducing as one of his "fundamental convictions" of social work that "the normally competent individual is the best judge of his own interests and must make his own decisions and work out his own problems,"[66] but the poor were apparently not considered competent. One writer claimed that 93% of families receiving Aid to Dependent Children needed "additional services,"[67] and another went so far as to prefer a system of public assistance to one of insurance, on the grounds that public assistance, despite all its unpleasant concomitants of less-eligibility and investigation, also involved social work service, while social insurance did not.[68]

Requiring Services

Services became an integral part of the law in 1956. Probably there is no clearer indication of the way in which basic nature of the program had changed than the revision that was made of Section 401 of the Social Security Act, the section setting forth the purposes of the Aid to Dependent Children program. This was the year in which the parents and other caretakers of dependent children were officially recognized as recipients, and the name of the program changed from Aid to Dependent Children to Aid to Families with Dependent Children. Before that, no one had been quite sure whether these children still belonged to their parents or were, in the words of one writer, "wards of the community."[69] But while this change gave the parent or relative a stronger

103

position, the goals of the program were no longer simply to provide him with the money to care for his children. They were sociological goals, incumbent on the recipient.

The Section originally began:

> For the purpose of enabling each State to furnish financial assistance, as far as practical under the conditions, to needy dependent children, there is appropriated . . .

which clearly identifies the program as one of financial assistance. But the intent of Title IV, as amended in 1956, is plainly rehabilitative.

> For the purpose of encouraging the care of dependent children in their own homes, or in the homes of relatives by enabling each State to furnish financial assistance and other services, as far as is practicable under the conditions in such State, to needy dependent children and the parents or relatives with whom they are living, to help maintain and strengthen family life and to help such parents or relatives to attain the maximum self-support and personal independence consistent with the maintenance of continuing parental care and protection, there is hereby authorized . .

In 1962 regulations were introduced requiring a social study and a "case-plan" for all recipients of Aid to Families with Dependent children.

Social Control

Toward Control

That social workers did not realize the degree to which they were again beginning to impose their own culture and psychological findings on their clients, including the poor, who in order to get the grants to which they legally entitled had to become social work "clients," is shown by the reaction to an article I wrote at the time suggesting that this was happening.[70] I was held to have quoted writers out of context and this criticism had some merit for it was, in 1953, just these little "straws in the wind" that disclosed where social workers' beliefs were taking them. They still believed, or believed that they believed, in client self-determination. But within a very few years it could hardly be said that they did. More and more groups of people were held to be not capable of making their own decisions, and social workers began to discuss freely their "authority" and "the social control function in social work."[71]

It began as early as 1946, when Dorothy Hutchinson wrote of the unmarried mother, "in my opinion the majority of these mothers are unable, if not incapable, of making their own independent decisions without skilled casework services."[72] In 1952, Lionel Lane extended this to neglectful parents and by implication to all clients: "The client frequently is not in a position to evaluate his problem clearly by virtue of his own closeness to it."[73] During this period also, the proportion of grants which could be paid to a guardian or trustee, instead of direct beneficiaries, doubled.

Authority

The problem of the social worker's "authority" concerned a number of workers at that time. Both the concept and the word itself caused difficulties. Annie Lee Davis, for instance, derived the agency's "authority" over the client from its authority to provide a service[74] which is to use the word in quite a different sense. Originally the debate centered on the authority of the agency to protect children from abuse, and was supposed to be derived either from community assent [75] or from the skill of the social worker. Karl and Elizabeth de Schweinitz, writing of protective services for children, identified several different types of authority, including one that they called "inherent"[76] and saw as beneficial. But in public assistance, workers at first saw this authority (implicit in their determining the amount of the grant) as something to be wary of. In 1941, Eda Honwink wrote that the worker:

> stands in a position of tremendous control from the client's point of view . . . the client is so helpless economically, and sometimes also personally, that the worker has to foresee his defenselessness and be very careful not to take unconscious advantage of him[77]

Yet by 1954, this inherent authority was being seen as a legitimate casework tool and casework was described, under certain conditions, as a "particular, highly skilled form of the exercise of influence."[78]

Direct attacks on the principle of the right to assistance, which is closely tied to that of self-determination, were not too common, but there were some. The reintroduction in the California Law of a "suitable home" provision, which is antithetical to this right, was hailed by one prominent social worker as putting "casework back into ADC."[79] Another leader in the field seemed to take a positive delight, interpreting the Minnesota program as one of gratuities rather than rights.[80] The strongest words were those of Joseph Baldwin, who wrote:

> Rigid adherence to the principle of the unrestricted money payment as set forth in the regulations of the Social Security Administration prevents the kind of control that commonsense tells us is necessary in some cases.[81]

The "right to assistance" and the unrestricted money grant were still the law, but they had been modified in practice as well as in the announced purpose of the program. Before we go on to consider what happened next, let us consider briefly why these changes had taken place.

Notes

The Impact of Freud

[1] Norman O. Brown, *Life Against Death,* New York, 1959, P. 6.

[2] Martin Buber, *I and Thou,* translated by Ronald Gregor Smith, New York, 1937.

[3] Philip Klein, "Social Work," *Encyclopedia of the Social Sciences,* New York, 1930-1935, Volume 14, p. 168.

[4] Dorothy Kahn, "Conserving Human Values in Public Welfare Programs," Proceedings of the National Conference of Social Work, 1939, pp. 275-276

[5] F. H. Steininger, "Desertion and the A.D.C. Program," *Public Welfare,* (October 1947): 238.

[6] Gordon Hamilton, "The Underlying Philosophy of Social Casework," 1941, reprinted in Cora Kasius, Ed., *Principles and Techniques in Social Case Work,* p. 10.

[7] Philip Klein, "The Social Theory of Professional Social Work," in H. E. Barnes, Howard Becker and Frances Bennett Becker, Eds., *Contemporary Social Theory,* New York, 1940, p. 755.

[8] Virginia Robinson, *A Changing Psychology in Social Work,* Chapel Hill, N.C., 1930, pp. 1813-184.

The Principle of Self-Determination

[9] Bertha Reynolds, *Re-Thinking Social Case Work,* San Diego, 1938, p. 15.

[10] In 1958 social workers were urged to "reassert their earlier belief in the plasticity of man" (Ruth Ellen Lindenberg, "Hard to Reach: Client or Casework Agency?" *Social Work,* 3, 4 (October 1958): 29.

[11] Swithun Bowers, "Social Work and Human Problems," *Social Casework,* 35: 189.

[12] Gordon Hamilton, "Helping People: The Growth of a Profession," in *Social Work as Human Relations: Anniversary Papers of the New York School of Social Work and the Community Service Society of New York,* New York, 1949, p. 88.

[13] Florence Hollis, *Social Case Work in Practice: Six Case Studies,* New York, 1939, p. 5.

[14] Saul Bernstein, "Self-Determination, King or Citizen in the Realm of Values?" *Social Work,* 5, 1 (January, 1960): 8.

[15] Hamilton, "Helping People," p. 88.

[16] See Alan Keith-Lucas, "A Critique of the Principle of Client Self-Determination," *Social Work*, 8, 3 (July 1963): 66-71.

[17] Helen Harris Perlman, "Self-Determination: Reality or Illusion?" *Social Service Review*, 39 (1965): 410-421.

[18] Hollis, *Social Casework in Practice*, p. 8.

[19] Felix P. Biestek, "The Principle of Client Self-Determination," *Social Casework*, 32, (1951): 369-375. In 1978 Father Biestek and Clyde C. Gehrig published *Client Self-Determination in Social Work: A Fifty-Year History*, (Chicago), in which they attempted to show that the "principle" had been progressively refined. But by this time the principle had been so subordinated in practice that it remained only as a mild check on excesses of imposed treatment techniques. More realistic sources are *Values in Social Work: A Re-Evaluation*, Monograph IX in the series sponsored by the Regional Institute Program, ational Association of Social Workers, New York, 1967 and F. E. McDermott, Ed., *Self-Determination in Social Work*, London, 1975, which include between them all of the major articles in this field up to that time.

[20] Saul Bernstein, "King or Citizen," pp .3-8.

[21] Grace Marcus, "The Status of Social Case Work Today," in Fern Lowry, Ed., *Readings in Social Casework*, 1920-1938, New York, 1939, p. 130.

[22] Biestek, "Basic Values in Social Work," in *Values in Social Work*, 1967, p. 13.

[23] Lionel Trilling, *Freud and the Crisis of our Culture*, Boston, 1935, p .48.

[24] Biestek, "The Principle of Client Self-Determination," pp. 370-371.

[25] Ronald L. Simons, "Strategies for Exercising Influence," *Social Work*, 27 (1982): 273.

[26] Bertha M. Kraus, "The Role of Social Case Work in American Social Work," in Kasius, *Principles and Techniques*, p. 139.

Social Insurance and the Right to Assistance

[27] Alan Keith-Lucas, "A Local Act for Social Insurance in the Eighteenth Century," *Cambridge Law Journal*, 11, 2 (1952): 191-197.

[28] Ibid., p. 196. The bill was introduced by friends of the Rev. John Acland who had stated his views in a pamphlet entitled *A Plan for Rendering the Poor Independent on Public Contribution*.

[29] William Lewery Blackley, "National Insurance: A Cheap, Practical and Popular Means of Abolishing Poor Rates," 1878, reprinted in *Nineteenth Century Opinion*, p. 766.

[30] Figures quoted from Barbara Tuchman, *The Proud Tower*, Bantam Books, 1966, p. 478.

[31] Ernest Witte, "Who Speaks Now for the Child in Public Assistance?" *Child Welfare*. 33, 3 (March, 1954): 9.

[32] Wilbur J. Cohen, "Factors Influencing the Content of Federal Public Welfare Legislation," *Social Welfare Forum*, 1954, p. 210.

[33] *Howlett vs. State Social Security Commission*, 347 Mo.784 (1941).

[34] E. V. Hollis and A. L. Taylor, *Social Work Education in the United States*, New York, 1951, p. 205.

[35] Federal Security Agency, *Money Payments to Recipients of Old Age Assistance, Aid to Dependent Children and Aid to the Blind*, Washington, D.C., 1944, pp. 6.

[36] Ibid., p. 27.

[37] Karl de Schwenitz, *People and Process in Social Security*, Washington, D.C., 19848. p. 25.

[38] Arthur J. Altmeyer, "Ten Years of Social Security," in W. Haber and W. J. Cohen, Eds., *Readings in Social Security*, New York, 1948, p. 84.

[39] A. Delafield Smith, *The Right to Life*, Chapel Hill, 1955, p. 2.

[40] A. Delafield Smith, "Community Prerogative and the Legal Rights and Freedom of the Individual," *Social Security Bulletin*, 9, 8 (Aug. 1946): 6.

[41] Smith, *The Right to Life*, p. 7.

[42] Smith, "Community Prerogative," ibid., p. 8.

[43] A "suitable home" provision authorized the local welfare department to deny or terminate a grant of assistance if the home was considered unsuitable for the rearing of a child. Such a finding, made without judicial process, was supposed to be followed by protective action in the courts to remove the child. In actual fact it often meant that the child was left in the home without a grant to support him. For a description of this provision in one State, see Maxine Board Virtue, *Study of the Basic Structure of Children's Services in Michigan*, Ann Arbor, 1953, p. 68.

[44] This was the famous "Jenner Amendment," actually an amendment to the Revenue Act of 1951, which forbade the publication of the names of recipients for "commercial or political purposes" but allowed for it in general.

[45] There was a welter of articles in periodicals attacking public assistance from 1947 to 1952. A bibliography of that time lists the following within an eighteen-month period.

"I Say Relief is Ruining Families," *Saturday Evening Post*, (September 1950).
"The Relief Chiselers are Stealing Us Blind," ibid. (September 1951).
"The Spreading State of Welfare," *Fortune* (February 1952).

"Chicago's Relief Revolution," *Reader's Digest* (February 1952).
"Broken Lives and Dollar Patches," *Nation's Business*, (March 1950).
"Seedbeds of Socialism — No. 1. The Federal Security Agency," (August 1950).
"When It Pays to Play Pauper," ibid., (September 1950).

Responsibility and the Social Norm

[46] Grace Marcus, *The Nature of Service in Public Assistance Administration*, Washington, D.C., 1947, p. 31.

[47] Jane Hoey, "The Significance of the Money Payment in Public Assistance," *Social Security Bulletin*, 7, 9 (September 1944):4.

[48] Jane Hoey, quoted by Josephine Gandelman, "Care of Children in Their Own Homes," *Round-Up*, Proceedings of the Southwest Regional Conference, American Public Welfare Association, Fort Worth, Texas, 1949), p. 64.

[49] Ruth Smalley, "The Relation of the Social Welfare Process to the Purpose of a Public Assistance Program," paper given to the New York Conference on Social Welfare, 1948.

[50] Kenneth Pray, *Social Work in a Revolutionary Age and Other Papers*, Philadelphia, 1948, p. 250.

[51] Jeanette Regensburg, "Reaching Children Before the Crisis Comes," *Social Casework*, 34 (1954): 106.

[52] Cora Kasius (Ed.), *A Comparison of Diagnostic and Functional Casework Concepts*, New York, 1950, p. 12.

[53] Gordon Hamilton, "The Underlying Philosophy of Social Casework," in Cora Kasius, *Principles and Techniques in Social Casework: Selected Articles 1940-1950*, New York, 1950, p. 12. The phrase which Hamilton used originally appeared in a review of her book, *The Theory and Practice of Social Case Work*, New York, 1940, and Florence Hollis, *Social Case Work in Practice: Six Case Studies*, New York, 1939. These were the two most widely-acclaimed books by "diagnostic" writers as reviewed by Isabelle K. Carter in *Social Forces*, 19 (1948): 137. Carter's review is popularly supposed to have prompted Hamilton's address, originally given at the National Conference of Social Work in 1941. This address was a somewhat intemperate attack on the "Functional" Schools and made

reconciliation of the two points of view almost impossible for the ensuing twenty years.

[54] Gordon Hamilton, "Basic Concepts in Social Work," in Fern Lowry (Ed.), *Readings in Social Case Work, 1920-1938,* New York, 1939, p. 156, quoting Ruth Benedict, *Patterns of Culture,* Boston, 1934, p. 258.

[55] Mary Antoinette Cannon, "Guiding Motives in Social work," in Cora Kasius (Ed.), *New Directions in Social Work*, New York, 1954.

[56] Gordon Hamilton, "Helping People -- the Growth of a Profession," in *Social Work as Human Relations: Anniversary Papers of The New York School of Social Work and the Community Service Society of New York,* New York, 1949, p. 10.

[57] Charlotte Towle, *Common Human Needs,* Washington, D.C., 1945, p. 10.

[58] Regensburg, "Reaching Children," p. 111.

[59] Hamilton, "The Role of Social Casework in Social Policy," *Selected Papers in Casework, National Conference of Social Work*, 1952, p. 71.

[60] Ibid.

[61] Hamilton, "The Underlying Philosophy," p. 10.

[62] Alice Overton, "Serving Families Who 'Don't Want Help'," *Social Casework*, 34 (1953): 304-309.

[63] Louis J. Lehrman, "The Logic of Diagnosis," *Social Casework*, 35 (1953):199.

[64] Bertha Reynolds, *Social Work and Social Living,* New York, 1951, p. 109.

[65] Annie Lee Davis, *Children Living in Their Own Homes*, Washington, D.C., p. 34.

[66] Herbert Bisno, *The Philosophy of Social Work*, p. 96.

[67] Constance M. Swander, "A Study of Services Needed in a Public Assistance Program" Public Welfare, 5 (1947): 198.

[68] Marjorie J. Smith, "The Place of Services in the Public Assistance Program," *Public Welfare,* 8 (1952): 47.

Social Control

[70] Notes and comments by the Editor, "Casework Labeled Undemocratic," Social Service Review, 28 (1954): 205-206, in rebuttal of my "The Political Theory Implicit in Social Casework Theory," *American Political Science Review,* 67 (1953): 1079-1091. This article was particularly unacceptable to leaders in the social work field because of its defense of the minority functional school.

[71] The latter phrase is the title of an article by Robert K. Taylor in *Social Casework*, 39 (1958): 17-21.

[72] Dorothy Hutchinson, "Re-examination of some Aspects of Case Work Practice in Adoption," *Child Welfare League of America Bulletin*, 25, 7 (November 1946): 6.

[73] Lionel Lane, "The 'Aggressive' Approach to Preventive Casework with Children's Problems," *Social Casework*, 33 (1952): 65.

[74] Davis, *Children Living in Their Own Homes*, p. 34.

[75] I was one of the earliest to try to derive the authority of the protective agency from community assent, a theory I would now reject. See my "The Caseworker in Protective Case Work: Responsibility in the Approach," *Child Welfare League of America Bulletin*, 20, 2 (February 1941):1-4.

[76] Karl and Elizabeth de Schweinitz, "The Place of Authority in the Protective Function of the Public Welfare Agency," *Child Welfare League Bulletin*, 25, 7 (September 1946): 1-6. This paper was considered so important that it was reproduced in full in *Child Welfare*, 43 (1946): 286-291, eighteen years later.

[77] *Eda Houwink, The Place of Casework in the Public Assistance Program, Chicago, 1941,* pp. 8-9.

[78] Elliot Studt, "An Outline for Study of Social Authority Factors in Casework," *Social Casework*, 35 (1954): 238.

[79] Kermit Wiltse, "Social Casework Services in the Aid to Dependent Children Program," *Social Service Review*, 38 (1954): 176.

[80] *Analysis of Social Social Security Systems: Hearings Before A Subcommittee on Ways and Means, House of Representatives,* 1954, testimony of Jarle Leirfallom and John W. Poor, pp. 814-817.

[81] Joseph Baldwin, "I Do Believe," *Louisiana Welfare*, 13 (1953).

Toward Retrenchment: Protection of Personal Privilege

The Erosion of a Right

Intervention Strategies for Aggressive Casework

It could be argued that the public was nowhere near ready for a welfare system based on rights; for justice, that is, rather than charity or the effort to reform the poor. Indeed, there is a good deal of evidence that many policies were established because of the somewhat questionable belief that a public opinion insisted on them.[1] But this does not account for the changes in social work thinking which we have detailed, a change which was symbolized by the new language that social work adopted. From about 1952, "aggressive" casework became a watchword, and from the early 1960s an almost military terminology was adopted. What social workers did, and still do today, was "intervene" and in doing so they employed "strategies."

Reasons for the Shift

There are at least eight possible explanations, all of which may be true in part.

1. That the nature of the poor had changed. It is true that in a period of affluence the poor are likely to be less competent as a group than are the poor in a period of depression and massive unemployment. Baldwin was of this opinion. He acknowledged that the right to assistance existed, but held that this right was born of the Depression and was, in 1953, no longer as valid as it had been in the Depression years.[2]

2. That social work's perception of people had changed. We have already noted how a "scientific" study of persons discloses them as extremely fallible beings and tends to concentrate on their failures. As we have seen, one worker saw in her clients not human beings, struggling with problems which were too big for them, but individuals with "uncontrolled impulsivity," "impairment in capacity to form relationships," and "ego and superego defectiveness" which "sharper social study methods and in-

creased psychiatric knowledge" had enabled her to detect.[3] Behavioral therapy sees persons as biologically and socially determined products whose reinforcers might be in need of altering. Analytical psychology sees man as basically irrational. On the other hand, science presumes that those who make use of it will behave rationally, creating an analog of the situation in which the Puritans saw Original sin in the unsuccessful and Grace accorded to themselves. Clients were seen as irrational, but social workers entirely rational.

3. That the sense of common human vulnerability, so obvious in the Depression, was no longer there. No longer was the social worker likely to be the client of tomorrow. It is interesting that at the same time that America was beginning to exercise more control over the poor, Great Britain was establishing programs that minimized or even abolished the difference between the poor and the well-to-do. The British Family Allowance was paid to rich and poor alike and the National Health Service was free to all. The means test was virtually abolished. It may be that the British still felt a sense of common vulnerability, not so much economically, although rationing was still in effect, but as a result of their common experiences in the war. Prominent British social workers were insistent that the poor, as a group, did not need rehabilitative services. Dame Eileen Younghusband, for instance, wrote of public assistance clients in 1951, "The vast majority are, of course, self-determining and independent people who have no need of "welfare."[4] Barbara Wooten (later Baroness Wooten of Abinger), a sociologist, argued that everyone had the right to be free, "not only to make his own choices within the law and not only to disregard good advice, but free, also, if he wishes, to avoid having good advice thrust upon him."[5] She pointed out that "a high proportion of the unfortunate people concerned would never have experienced (social workers') attentions, had it not been for financial difficulties."[6]

4. That social workers had lost their sense of awe in the face of the new knowledge that analytic psychology had brought to them. What enabled the early Freudian social workers to accept the right to self-determination and the unrestricted money grant was both a sense of awe in the face of disturbing new theories of human motivation and their acceptance of Freud's psychic determinism. But psychic determinism cannot exist in an optimistic culture any more than the Puritans could accept that God's elec-

tion of some and not others followed no principle that they could understand; in which case man can "seek to please God only by the degree of his humility."[7] Persons, in the religious context, had to assure their own salvation, and in the social work context, regain their belief in the "plasticity of human nature." Otherwise, their tasks appeared hopeless.

5. That social workers were abandoning the view from the inside out that Freud had introduced, and were beginning to look at man from the outside in. This was to happen much more markedly when, a few years later, social work enlarged its scientific interests and began to rely on sociology and epidemiology as an explanation of man's behavior. But it began to happen with the adoption of ego-psychology. Science, in fact, despite that fact that it was given credit for the "inside-out" view, as we have seen, can never be happy with it, for the individual's perception is by nature personal and unscientific. Science finds it very difficult to treat man as the subject, as it were, of the sentence. Its findings are ontic rather than ontological or phenomenological: certain empirical measures of things rather than how they are perceived -- the difference between "Music is a vibrating string," and "Music is a Beethoven symphony." There was, and is, an existential "school" of social work, but it was, and is, very much in the minority.[8]

6. That social work cannot escape its own history. The desire to "do good" to others, to play what Barbara Wooten calls "the priestly, if not godlike role," persists whatever the current theory may be. We have not really moved very far from the ethos of the Charity Organization Society or the Christian Socialists. Social workers, she writes, even of those in Britain, who had by that time adopted many American ideas, "have an unfortunate heredity, and as with others in the same case, it is not easy for them wholly to shake off the baneful influence of their disreputable ancestors."[9]

7. That social work had become respectable and had allied itself with the prevailing culture. Gone was the radicalism of the 1930's and early 1940's when many social workers were, if not communists, at least critics of the economic system. Social work had become a "socially-sanctioned profession."[10]

8. That what had happened was the inevitable result of a Human-Positivist-Utopian world view, which always starts with a high estimate of persons but ends with having to control them.

Exceptions

It should not be thought that all social workers were caught in this problem. There were objectors, such as Alvin Schorr in his article, "The Tendency to Rx"[11] and David Soyer in his "The Right to Fail."[12] Biestek could still say, with patent sincerity, that "the dignity and worth of the human being is the supreme value in the social work hierarchy of value"[13] although there were different interpretations of how this should be implemented. The welfare system was less oppressive than it had been in the days of the Poor Law and the Workhouse. Several states maintained a strict "rights" program. Louisiana listed as the fundamental concepts under which it operated as:

- The unrestricted right to apply for public assistance when and as often as the client wishes.
- The right to have his eligibility established promptly and accurately.
- The right to obtain all the assistance for which he is eligible.
- The right to retain his personal dignity when applying for or receiving assistance.[14]

Nevertheless, in the 1960s it became apparent that the system did not appear as protective of human dignity as might be hoped. By 1969, in fact, Martin Eisman could write:

> It is through the process of making the individual dependent, insecure, intimidated, humiliated, unsafe and the like that the welfare department unwittingly strives toward what had become its main function: the destruction of dignity and self-respect.[15]

The Welfare Explosion and Revolt

The Services Solution

At the beginning of the 1960s, social workers and others persuaded Congress that the answer to the rising costs of welfare was more social services to those in need. There had been isolated experiments in intensive casework with welfare clients, which seemed to show an improvement in "more personally and socially effective or satisfactory behavior" on the part of clients.[16] Congress apparently generalized from these a belief that additional social services would reduce the number of people on relief. "Experience has shown," said the House Ways and Means Committee," that adequate trained personnel can be one of the largest factors in reducing ultimately the cost of public assistance programs."[17]

They could not have been more wrong. During the time from 1960 to 1968 the number of people on relief more than doubled, and 70% of this increase took place between 1964 and 1968.[18] The reasons for this have been debated at length. It can be shown that there is little correlation between the demand for assistance and more adequate welfare payments, although average payments did rise by about one-third during this time, but unevenly across the country. Daniel Moynihan believed that the rise could be ascribed to the progressive deterioration of the black family[19] but the rise was among both whites and blacks. Piven and Cloward discounted the actual effects of demonstrations by welfare clients, but concluded that the rise was a "political response to political disorder."[20]

What Happened

Two things had, in fact, happened. First, the poor had been discovered. In 1962 Michael Harrington published his *The Other America,*[21] and in 1964 Ben Bagdikian his *In The Midst of Plenty,*[22] only two of many books on the subject. It is perhaps significant that neither of these two authors were social scientists. They were journalists.

Second, there was a new feeling for the rights of any group that had formerly been denied them. These groups were not only blacks, although their rights were a starting point, but women, students, children, youth in general, other racial or ethnic minorites, more recently homosexuals,[23] and, specifically, the poor. On some occasions these groups worked together. It was an informal coalition of welfare clients, black activists, and young welfare workers, most of them women, who disrupted both the 1968 and the 1969 meetings of the National Conference on Social Welfare, refusing to allow the planned program to be implemented and in effect holding the delegates hostage.[24]

The War on Poverty

Whether the government "responded" to the threat of disorder, as Piven and Cloward would have it, or whether it had some conviction about rights themselves, the outcome was President Johnson's "War on Poverty." The two parts of this which probably had the greatest impact on the poor were the Community Action Program, which sought to help the poor develop political power, and the Legal Services program, which helped the poor both discover and implement their legal rights.

The Community Action Program enunciated a new principle, comparable to self-determination. This was the "maximum feasible participation" of the poor in programs concerning them. Many such programs were led by activists, described by some as "left over from the civil rights movement."[25] Theirs was a confrontation model.

In some areas something like an alternative local government emerged, bypassing and bringing pressure on the established power structure, which was resented by that establishment. It seemed to some as if the federal government was deliberately undermining local governments and nurturing organizations not unlike Russian soviets, and indeed there is some evidence that the Office of Economic Opportunity did not believe that the poor would ever attain power unless local government was reformed.[26] Something of the same argument was leveled against the Legal Services program; many local governments found themselves sued by the poor.

Public Assistance Regulations

But probably the biggest change in how the poor were actually treated came about through the establishment of the National Welfare Rights Organization and its local counterparts and affiliates.[27] What the poor discovered, for the first time, was the law of public assistance. Public assistance manuals, previously only workbooks for the public assistance worker, were distributed widely.

The excessive individualization of public assistance regulations intended at first to be flexible enough to meet any poor person's need (most manuals were hundreds of pages in length) had been used also to exclude anyone who could conceivably be ineligible. But its worst fault was that clients did not know to what they were entitled or what they must do to qualify for asssistance. This, according to two lawyers, "invited arbitrary and whimsical exercises of power," "constitutes the very thing to be prevented by the idea of government of laws and not of men," and "flies in the face of basic requirements of proper classification."[28] A great deal of the increase in the welfare roles was undoubtedly due to the fact that the poor now knew their rights. Yet even in 1980 it has been estimated that less than half of those eligible actually applied for various forms of public assistance.[29]

The Courts

The poor also brought their rights to the attention of the courts, and thereby discovered new rights. Legal Services and the American Civil Liberties Union were able, during the 1960s, to have declared unconstitutional a number of residence requirements for relief, the "employable mother," "man in the house," and "substitute parent" rules used in many states,[30] arbitrary termination of relief, and nighttime raids without a warrant.[31]

On the legislative side, one important new right was established, but only on a means-test basis, that of medical care by the enactment of Medicaid in 1964. In 1964 also, the Food Stamp program was made permanent. The original purpose was more to find a way of disposing of stocks of food that the Department of Agriculture had accumulated as a way of subsidizing farmers than as a gesture to the poor. However, it rapidly became somewhat of a favored program, partly because it was "relief in kind" rather than in cash, partly because it required some expenditure by the poor, and partly because it was, at first, based on a simple income basis without a lot of individualizing provisions.[32]

Separation of Services

The most significant change, however, in the philosophy of the welfare system was at first an administrative one: the separation of financial assistance from the provision of social services. The poor were in need of social services, but they were no longer to be a "captive audience" more or less forced to accept services by the fact of their financial dependence. They could, for the most part, choose what social services they desired.[33] Social services were no longer to be a means of getting them "off welfare," or, what some had held them to be, a substitute for financial assistance. Moreover, the poor had a right to the social services they desired.

Social services were seen by some writers to be much like public utilities, which one might expect to find either provided to everyone, such as police or fire protection, or to be purchased, like electricity or gas. Where a family had insufficient funds to purchase the services it desired, it would either be provided with the money, or scrip would be issued which it could use at will.

In 1968 the Department of Health, Education and Welfare established a Task Force on the organization of Social Services, which came out in favor of using "economic market mechanisms" in the distribution of services. It recommended a grant-in-aid to be paid directly to individuals, "giving them a claim on a share of services."[34] This concept was sometimes called the "Warehouse Concept"; services were seen as commodities in a warehouse, which could be ordered at will.[35]

Access to Services

In the view of the leaders of the "client revolution," access to services was likely to be denied by the authorities. In general, two remedies were found.

One was the "Storefront" agency or Neighborhood Center, which challenged the Welfare Department's practices (as one worker put it, "Any way you cut it, they [the Welfare Department] are the enemy"). In one case at least, a center protected a mother from a charge of child neglect by presenting evidence that her "child-rearing efforts had been stymied by consistent underbudgeting for more than a year."[36]

Another was the employment of paraprofessional, "indigenous" workers from the same culture as the recipients of welfare who acted as "expediters" to insist that an individual or a family obtain the services they desired.[37]

At the same time, the National Association of Social Workers established an Ad Hoc Committee on Advocacy, and advocacy for the poor became an accepted and indeed mandated role for the professional social worker. He or she was to be "his client's supporter, his advisor, his champion, and if need be his representative in his dealings with the court, the police and the social agency."[38]

Results

The "War on Poverty" did not abolish poverty. An assessment in 1976 estimated that there had been substantial progress in overcoming poverty measured in absolute terms — that is, reaching a minimum level of well-being without comparing it with the average standard of living of the populace as a whole. However, there was no progress either in the ability of people to do without government help or in the incidence of relative poverty. In other words, what had taken place was a general improvement in living standards and a more generous welfare system, but no redressing of economic inequality.[39]

That the "War on Poverty" petered out was due to a number of factors. There was considerable conservative backlash. The end of the Vietnam War removed one of the principal causes of civic unrest. Popular philosophy turned from concern for others to the search for personal self-fulfillment. Mr. Moynihan counseled "benign neglect." And the profession which, by and large, would be responsible for on-going services to the poor was itself in disarray.

"Casework is Dead"

Does Casework Work?

Until the early 1960s casework and social work had been almost synonymous terms. Casework, moreover, in its predominant "diagnostic" model, was largely concerned with the treatment of personal maladjustments to society and personal pathology. Florence Hollis published her *Social Casework: A Psychosocial Therapy* in 1964, although Helen Harris Perlman had more or less healed the breach between the diagnostic and functional schools by her acceptance of the concept of Will in her *Social Casework: A Problem Solving Process*,[41] and Anita Faatz had added greatly to the understanding of how people are helped in her *Nature of Choice in Casework Process*.[42]

But casework service had failed to rehabilitate the poor and doubts began to arise as to whether it was also effective in altering human behavior.[43] These doubts culminated in an article in 1973 which reviewed eleven studies, mostly from the 1950s and 1960s, and came to the conclusion that:

> not only has professional casework failed to demonstrate it is effective, but lack of effectiveness appears to be the rule rather than the exception across several categories of clients, problems, situations, and types of casework.[44]

It should be pointed out, however, that casework in this article is equated throughout with psychotherapy, and the measure of effectivness is almost universally "more acceptable behavior," measured by court appearances and so forth, or rather vague criteria such as "family functioning." A question, not discussed in length here, might be asked at this point. Should casework, a personal helping method, ever have undertaken the tasks on which it was being judged. Paul Halmos, in his *Faith of the Counsellors*, had written of the "mirage of results."[45] Is it possible that these results are more existential than readily measurable by available, empirical data?

But casework had clearly been expected to produce measurable results. Scott Briar thought that it had failed to do so because its knowledge base was too restricted.[46] Nathan Cohen wrote that "in a period calling for rapid social change there was a need for a theory in casework that would deal with a changing individual as well as a changing society."[47] By 1960, "it was becoming clear that our approach to social problems was fragmented, with too much focus on the individual as the entrepreneur and as the cause of his own predicament,[48] thereby recognizing that we had not moved as far as we thought from the Capitalist-Puritan ethic. Mr. Cohen also echoed a common criticism: that casework helped people adjust to society, including its oppressive features, instead of helping them change it, and called for a theory which "would differentiate deviance as pathology from deviance as healthy revolt against unfair and undemocratic social conditions."[49] The need for casework was defended by Helen Harris Perlman in two articles,[50] and by Alvin Schorr, who called it "the real thing."[51]

The Ascendancy of Action

But the action was with Community Organization. And the leaders in Community Organization were not principally social workers. They were lawyers, social scientists of various stripes, journalists, and political leaders. One prominant writer, Harry Specht, even doubted that in the social scene of the future a professional social worker would find a job.[52] Nor, when professional social workers joined the movements that were underway, had they anything much to contribute to them. "Social work," wrote Martin Rein, "by itself has almost nothing to contribute to the reduction of the interrelated problems of unemployment, poverty, and dependency." [53] Anita Faatz, from the functional school of social casework, did indeed suggest that perhaps what social work might have to offer was help to the individual in making use of the opportunities that were opening up for him and believed that social work alone had some understanding of the process that would be involved.

Social workers as Community Change Agents

But social workers whose main concern had been with the treatment of pathology tended to deny what they had learned about human growth and change, and with it some of their long-held values. They learned from such writers as Saul Alisky and Herbert Aptheker [55] techniques of confrontation and disruption and practiced them in their work. Articles on disruptive tactics appeared in professional periodicals. As one of these put it:

> As long as this country participates in unjust wars of conquest and does not provide the resources needed to deal with domestic crises of racism, poverty and other social injustices, all professionals will face the dilemma of either working through institutions they believe may be unable to overcome social rot or participating in their destruction. [56]

The author, Harry Specht, calls this an "awful choice" but still warns against "guerilla" tactics. There must be a minimum of order.

There is some question as to whether many social workers who participated in some of the movements of the day did so within their function as social workers at all. It was almost as if Porter R. Lee had not distinguished cause and function in 1929.[57] Martin Rein said of these workers that their activities were "marginal to their professional tasks."[58]

There were two possible solutions to this dilemma. One was to extend the boundaries of social work, or alternatively, to create a new, more inclusive profession of "human service professional" to deal with social problems. The "social worker" of the future would only minimally be involved with individual problem-solving or therapy. In fact, he or she might not be involved in it at all. The Dean of one school of social work hoped and foresaw that by the year 2000 ninety percent of social work students would be committed to organization, administration, research, and policy and only ten percent to direct practice, a complete reversal of the present distribution. Direct service was thought to be out of date. "We must commit ourselves," he wrote, "to a gradual phasing out of those professional services with roots in Nineteenth Century individualism."[59]

Casework Is Not Dead

It might be remarked that social work is unlikely to follow this prescription. Although there are more students in research, policy and administration than there were when his statement was written (in 1969), the majority of social work students are still in clinical practice. Indeed it is more and more fashionable for social workers to set themselves up in private psychotherapeutic practice, thereby, despite some concern for insurance schemes that would not limit them to a middle- or high-income clientele, more or less turning their backs on the poor.[60] It is hard in fact to find much common ground between the clinical social worker and the social planner or administrator. In many schools of social work they pursue entirely different curricula.

The "Knowledge Explosion"

How Big An Explosion?

The other solution to the apparent failure of social casework to change people's behavior was to react to what was known as "the knowledge explosion." The existence of this "explosion" is so much an article of belief in social work today that it may appear almost blasphemous to throw doubt on its reality. Undoubtedly there was a great proliferation of social studies, using for the most part sophisticated statistical methodology. There was also a plethora of new formulations and models. There were new, conflicting, and sometimes helpful insights into human behavior and some validation of what was already known through practice. There was a great deal of relabeling and reconceptualization, as well as new techniques, mostly of a manipulative nature. But whether very much more became known about the human predicament or how the lot of the poor can be alleviated or a more just and productive society constructed is, I suggest, open to doubt.

Indeed one maverick writer, Elizabeth Salomon, saw the increasingly positivistic movement in social work as actually restricting social work's knowledge in that it disclaimed intuitive understanding and the whole range of man's "spiritual and moral nature."[61] She pointed out that science dealt in abstractions and quotes the psychiatrist, Erik Erickson, as saying that, "This term [reality or objective reality] more than any other, represents the Cartesian strait jacket that we have imposed on our model of man."[62]

There may have been a need to think of all this knowledge as new, but I would suggest that what really happened was that social workers gave up their reliance on a single discipline, analytical psychology, and borrowed widely from others: sociology, behavioral learning theory, psychology, epidemiology, management theory, systems analysis, and so on. They saw themselves as eclectic social scientists. Research became the source of all knowledge; we have already seen that results that are not measurable could be held to be illusory. Practitioners were at first exhorted to make use of the findings of social research,[63] but then to integrate research with practice, so that every case became both an attempt to help and an exercise in research. By 1981, in fact, Joel Fischer could announce a "revolution" in social work, albeit a quiet one, in which social workers will give up their reliance on "vague" [a favorite word of his] traditional theories, in favor of "clear, specific, systematic, and rational criteria" to select the knowledge they use in practice.[64] The "new breed" of social worker will be "a scientific practioner."[65] He or she will use largely those techniques that have been shown to be effective.

Effective for What?

It is noticeable that Fischer does not ask, "effective for what?" and that the two models he believes to have shown their effectiveness are behavior modification and cognitive change procedures, which he sees as closely allied. Both involve the social worker deliberately changing something she sees as irrational or undesirable. This may or may not give much rein to the client's own feelings or aspirations. But he adds to his list of proven techniques structuring of the encounter (though with little discussion of which structures are helpful), and then, rather surprisingly, the "interpersonal skills" of "empathy, warmth and genuineness" of which he writes that:

> Although the evidence in this area is neither as elegant nor consistent as in the other three, it is sufficient to suggest that these communication skills are important for social work practice . . . Indeed, a body of some ten experimental studies show that practitioners who communicate higher levels of empathy, warmth and genuineness are also more effective in their use of several behavioral procedures.[66]

Empathy is indeed a skill, but "warmth" and "genuineness" can only be measured by how they appear to an outsider. To conceptualize them as skills to be employed would appear to raise questions of how they have been defined. To decide to be warm or genuine might sound to some a contradiction.

Indeed the "scientific practitioners" with their emphasis on behavior, their selection of techniques that have proved to be effective (however empathic, warm, and genuine they may be), are not too far philosophically from the Charity Organization worker. They want what is good for the client, what they believe will make him happy or productive, and they define it largely in terms of middle-class culture and ethics. Lip service is frequently given to the notion that intervention will be in keeping with the client's own goals, but this is easy to lose sight of in results-oriented practice, especially with difficult or resistant clients, or those whose goals seem to the worker to be destructive. It is perhaps significant that in "the social work revolution" there is no re-thinking of client's rights, only a statement that what is proposed does "maintain the basic values, ethics and philosophy of social work" which are described as "the profession's intrinsic humanistic orientation."[67]

Manipulation and Self-Determinism

One concept that has been employed to mitigate the control factor in this type of social work is to insist that manipulative techniques should only be used when there is mutual agreement between client and social worker about the tasks to be accomplished. This is cited by Simons who describes a number of "strategies," some of them amounting to rather subtle trickery, in which persons can be influenced to make wise decisions.[68] One of the examples given is that of a teen-ager quitting school to take a low-paying job and one wonders what mutual agreement on goals were involved here. Salzberger holds that a client's right to self-determination is preserved when the plan worked out by social worker and client is "most representative of the client's aspirations."[69] This might be difficult to determine, but it does free self-determination from too rigid a reliance upon whim. The article adds that "what is especially odious about manipulation is that it is stealthy."[70]

The other articles also deal with the client's self-determination. One which questions the "medical metaphor" states:

> The proposal presented here contends that a caseworker cannot take responsibility for making a client's decision. The worker can, however, affect such decisions by limiting or expanding the client's choices or by changing the other information the client receives.[71]

One could wish that the author had omitted the word "limiting." The other returns to the concept of maximum feasible participation"

> The solutions are not pre-determined by the worker, but are worked out jointly by the worker and client according to the client's understanding and capacities. This is the true and enduring portion of the myth of helping and one which must be nurtured.[72]

These comments do not refer specifically to the poor. Nevertheless the poor remain the greater part of the social work load, and are the least likely to enter into voluntary contracts to achieve tasks of their own selection.

Erosion

Despite these statements, the gains of the 1960s soon began to erode, although some progress had been made. The separation of services from financial aid was unmandated in 1976, and to some extent this was seen as desirable. Studies showed that when these functions were integrated there was greater utilization of services. How many of these were truly voluntary it would be hard to say.[73] "Maximum feasible participation" had early developed its skeptics, not only among politicians[74] but among social workers.[75]

126

The "War on Poverty" more or less fizzled out, partly because of white and middle-class backlash, but partly because the profession most intimately concerned was essentially humanist, positivist, and utopian and still tended to see the poor in terms of the "medical metaphor" as those in need of rehabilitation.

Alternatives to the "Welfare Mess"

Now What?

The attempt to establish a dignified income maintenance program had clearly failed. Its rights features were seen by some as an illusion. As Hess put it:

> The notion that welfare is a "right" which somehow makes it different from charity may be of poetic interest but surely is not of any pragmatic interest. It simply is not a right. It is a grant, carefully and purposively administered not by some blind goddess of justice but by very open-eyed political operatives and employees of the state.[76]

His solution is self-help, both by developing skills among the poor and providing them with surplus tools and perhaps some capital. He even suggests a return to private charity for the incapacitated, pointing out that much of this will come from the former poor. This is reminiscent of Thomas Chalmers, but is quoted here as a sign of disillusionment with a so-called "rights" system based on a means test.

During the 1960s and 1970s many theoreticians dreamed of a better system and looked in general to Europe for ideas. While we are not concerned here with the logistics of various systems or even their effect on the economy as a whole (which does affect their feasibility), their concept of the causes of poverty and the relationship between the poor and the rich are of interest. Historically we have had systems based on the belief that while some poor deserve relief, others do not: assistance to the deserving only. We have had systems based on the belief that the poor are lacking in will-power or are ignorant, which rely either on measures that make being poor even more unpleasant, such as less-eligibility and pauperism, or attempt to control or reform the poor. We have systems based on the belief that poverty is largely the result of misfortunes and either should be insured against or entitle the person to relief if he does not himself have the resources to cope with the disaster (old age, physical handicap, loss of parental support). We have systems

127

that have tried to prevent destitution by providing work, and therefore wages, or to encourage self-help projects. We have systems that have believed dependence on others to be an enervating thing, and therefore demand work, even if there is no real work to be done, in payment of relief.

All these systems, with the exception of social insurance and perhaps some work-relief and self-help programs, identify the poor and subject them to various tests and investigations to establish the fact of their poverty. The poor are placed in a category which is at the same time subordinate, subject to regulation and often disdain from those who are not so classified, and yet in some ways favored, so that there is constant suspicion that they are claiming to be poor when in fact they are not. In such circumstances it is very hard for them to retain much dignity or to consider themselves fully citizens of the state. They are a group, a class, for whom the rules are different. They are "on welfare" and the word is even used as an adjective, "welfare mothers."

Three Basic Alternatives

Providing that a country wants to do something about this situation and at the same time provide its poorest citizens with the necessities of life, to say nothing of a share in the national wealth (a concept rarely heard in America)[77] there are basically three devices it can use.

It can make a grant to everyone who undertakes a certain responsibility, usually the rearing of children, as in most European countries and British dominions such as Canada and New Zealand. This is technically known as a demogrant, is paid to rich and poor alike, and the costs recovered by what the British call "claw-back," i.e., a progressive income tax. Or the country can assure a minimum income for everybody by use of a negative income tax. Or third, it can expand the services that the community offers to all people without individualized payment on their part, as in the British Health Service or in American public schools and public recreation.

None of these services discriminate against the poor; even the phrase "income transfers" is somewhat invidiously applied to them. They are more in the nature of pooled efforts. Their "cost," too, is somewhat illusory. What is at stake is the amount that the wealthy are willing to contribute, not so much to the poor, but to the common good.

These programs were debated at length in the literature of the 1960s and 1970s.[78] Only three versions received national attention.

By far the most radical and humane of these was Senator McGovern's proposal for a "social dividend" of $1000 per annum for every individual in the country, which combined the idea of a demogrant with that of a guaranteed minimum income. It met with an overwhelming negative response and Senator McGovern himself soon disclaimed it. People could not understand granting Mr. Rockefeller $1000 even if the state recouped many times that in income taxes. One Republican advertisement claimed that it would put more than half of the country on welfare, which in one sense it would have done, since there are more people with incomes below the average than above it. But the connotations of "welfare" obscured its democratic intent.

Nixon's "Family Allowance Plan" introduced in 1969 did appear to guarantee a minimum income. It sought to equalize welfare payments throughout the country -- eleven years later AFDC grants still varied from an average of $88 in Mississippi to $431 in California -- and for the first time included single persons and the working poor. But it was a "welfare" program, means-tested, and included heavy incentives for people to work. It might be noted that those who are required to work, or offered unrefusable incentives to do so, are largely the mothers of fatherless children. At the same time that President Nixon was proposing that all welfare mothers work, he vetoed a bill that would have provided day care for many more children, reputedly on the grounds that it would provide free day care for some middle-class families.

Nixon's Family Assistance Plan was never enacted into law. It was attacked both by conservatives and liberals, the former because it provided something like a guaranteed income, the latter because of its low income limits and its work requirements. Nixon, indeed, did not press for it. Some of its income maintenance features were in fact taken care of by the Food Stamp Plan, which eliminated many of the more recondite eligibility requirements but was definitely relief in kind rather than in cash. This controlled, or rather tried to control, the expenditures of the poor, and made their poverty obvious at the check-out line.

Carter also promised "welfare reform" and failed to enact it. His proposals did contain one new idea, the responsibility of the federal government to provide employment for those able and willing to work.[79] He actually budgeted for 725,000 federal jobs.[80] Otherwise his proposals were not essentially different from Nixon's. Universal health insurance was accepted as an ideal, but postponed until the economy could recover.

What Was Left

We were left at the end of the decade with the means-tested, highly unpopular AFDC program, which had lost many of its "rights" features. The separation of relief from services had been unmandated. From the

129

early 1970s selected jurisdictions had been permitted to require welfare recipients to work as a condition of obtaining relief, a very different matter from providing jobs for the unemployed. The results of these experiments had been discouraging. Working for relief, popularly known as "workfare" was shown, in one study at least, not to have enhanced the employability of welfare recipients, which was one of its announced goals. Nor did it lower welfare costs in any significant way. In general heads of households who were able to work wanted to do so but the jobs were not available.[81] What "workfare" programs do is to make welfare more palatable to those who pay taxes to provide it, fifty-six percent of whom, according to a study made in 1978, believe that the need for welfare is due to the personal failure of the would-be recipient and that most welfare recipients are malingerers.[82]

Old people and the disabled were now served by the Supplemental Security Income, a means-tested federal program which did at least set national standards and did divorce financial assistance from the demand to accept social services. "Welfare" came to mean largely the families where the father was incapacitated, unemployed, absent, or unacknowledged. There had been some progress in meeting two of the basic needs of this group through the Food Stamp Plan and through Medicaid, both on a means-tested basis, and both programs giving relief in kind rather than in cash, which may account for the mild popularity they enjoyed. Indeed by the end of the decade "in kind" programs, including school lunches and subsidized housing were costing twice as much as was assistance in cash.[83]

Both Medicaid and Food Stamps grew enormously in the decade. Both, too, were administratively vulnerable to considerable abuse. Food stamps in particular constituted a second currency, which could be counterfeited or sold on the black market. Secretary Simon called the program a "haven for the cheats and the rip-off artists."[84] Recipients were, it might be remarked, modest in their cheating. They probably cheated rather less than those who with less excuse falsified income tax and expense accounts. The most serious cheating came from racketeers, just as the really serious abuses in the Medicaid program came from the doctors and the hospitals who provided the service.

Nevertheless, by 1980 something of a floor had been placed beneath most of the poor -- a somewhat shaky floor, perhaps, but some assurance that most had no need to be without adequate food or medical services.[85]

The Conservative Reaction

Back to the Poor Law

The actions of the Reagan administration that came into power in 1980 were not simply an attempt to cut back on welfare programs in order to reduce federal spending or a shift from "butter" to "guns" as a national priority. They were an attempt to return America to the principles of the Poor Law. Principles that were current a hundred or two hundred years ago and had long been abandoned in any civilized country were refurbished. These include:

1. Assistance to the deserving only. Two apologists for Reagan's philosophy identified the "truly poor," whom Reagan saw as the only persons who should be helped, as those "unfortunate persons who through no fault of their own have nothing but public funds to turn to in order to secure a minimal standard of living" and also wrote of "those who deserve welfare."[86]

2. A minimal standard of living. Not only did Reagan reject any concept of equalizing income, however slightly, but he asked only that "truly needy Americans should be able to survive."[87] This is a standard lower than even the "minimum health and decency" that was written into many AFDC laws and regulations. Any idea that people living on this standard are not likely to be able to show much initiative was ignored. Indeed, he believed the opposite. His apologists quoted a study, made perhaps significantly by the United States Chamber of Commerce, that shows that "guaranteeing a level of income higher than necessary to meet basic needs reduces a person's incentive to work."[88] The key phrase here is "basic needs." The article translates these into minimal needs for survival.

3. The concept of a "safety-net" instead of a floor on which one can stand. The problem with a safety net is that one cannot stand on it. One can only lie down. A "safety net" is the surest way of ensuring a permanent underclass.

4. Less-eligibility. "Benefit levels should be adequate to meet basic needs at all times but should not compete with an area's wages for those who are able-bodied."[89] While this is reasonable when one is dealing with possibly able-bodied persons, it further handicaps the handicapped.

5. Return of welfare decisions to the local level and to private charity, both of which have been notoriously arbitrary and

moralistic in the past. These decisions will, the administration believes, "more perfectly reflect the popular will." They will also be "presumably more appropriate."[90] Any idea that they may be more prejudiced, more unjust, or more politically oriented, unless they operate under nationally agreed guidelines and constraints, is ignored. Yet history has shown that only a national government can balance local enthusiasms sufficiently to ensure justice. Piven and Cloward believe that the basic motive for returning decisions to the local level is to fragment any protest movement.[91]

6. A return to the belief that people will stop being poor if only being poor is made uncomfortable enough. California has reintroduced the Workhouse and "indoor relief," although only for its residual "General Relief" category, largely of single men. Nevertheless, experience shows that a measure of this sort applied to one category of the poor tends to be expanded to others.

7. Belief that most welfare clients are cheats or malingerers. While the article examined here specifically says that "the majority of welfare recipients are not cheats. They are honest people who rely on federal transfer programs to help them meet burdensome expenses" and, "not all of them are destitute,"[92] the picture is clearly that of a group of people taking unfair advantage of benefits. Reagan himself delighted in stories of Food Stamp recipients who bought cigarettes with their stamps or Chicago's "Welfare Queen." But little is said of those who cheat on income taxes, who are, if an article in *Time* is to be believed, largely "white middle-class, middle-and upper-income people like doctors, lawyers, the self-employed, landlords, people trading on the stock-market." These are persons who have far less reason to cheat but do, by some estimates, to the tune of one-quarter the amount owed. This is far more, in fact, than the total cost of all "welfare" programs put together.[93] One might ask why it is so much more wicked to take a little more of the public treasury than one is entitled to, than it is to fail to accept one's fair share in contributing to that treasury.

The Abandonment of Commutative Justice

One can only believe this if one abandons the concept of commutative justice altogether. The poor, it is apparently believed, have no rights, legal or moral, to any part of the national wealth, because they have not earned it in the market place. Wealth belongs, individually, to those who

132

earn it. This is believed to be a "natural" right[94] which, in philosophy, usually means one derived from the Almighty. People agree to relinquish some of their right to spend their income as they individually wish when they direct the government to perform certain collective functions for them. The poor are therefore entirely at the mercy of the compassion of the rich.

The whole of this philosophy is summed up in George Gilder's *Wealth and Poverty*, where it is given a strongly moral connotation as well as a great deal of economic theory of a somewhat unproved nature. Reagan is reported to have been so much impressed by it that he gave a copy to every member of his administrative team.

Gilder believes that the solution to poverty lies in three things: *work*, "the poor must not only work, they must work harder than the classes above them"[95]; *the maintenance of monogamous marriage*, "husbands work 50 percent harder than bachelors of comparable age, education and skills," and "once a family is headed by a woman it is almost impossible for it to greatly raise its income"[96]; and *faith*, "faith in man, faith in the future, faith in the rising returns of giving" (by which he means the capitalist system, which he believes to be based on giving), "faith in the mutual benefits of trade, and faith in the providence of God."[97] He is careful not to blame the poor. "The poor choose leisure not because of moral weakness, but because they are paid to do so"[98] by moral liberals (he really thinks liberalism is immoral). However, his stereotype of families on welfare who are committing no legal fraud and are therefore being indulged by the system is:

> welfare mothers who live and bear children of dubious paternity with a succession of men working from time to time in the economy of the street, or those who dabble in prostitution, sharing apartments with other welfare mothers while leaving the children with a forty-five year old grandmother upstairs, who is receiving payments for "disability from a sore back."

He would almost seem to excuse the "more honest and ambitious" who tell the truth about their cirumstances, "try to leave the welfare culture" (i.e., are ineligible) and so "do not come into the reach of welfare computers."[99] He obviously has no conception of what it is like to be poor, or Black (he consideres racial discrimination to be a myth), or indeed of the difference between the social conditions of the last century and this.

Basis for a Just Society

What is lacking in these pronouncements, other than compassion, is any sense of the necessity for sharing any of the benefits of our economy. It is a "dog eat dog" society, despite comforting theories about "trickle-down" effects. Although Americans, by and large, are very generous people and there are many instances of shared efforts to help the poor in local communities (the United Fund is an American invention), the concept has never found a place in its economic theory.

In an article which rather unfortunately uses the phrase "welfare state" with its negative implications of cradle-to-grave security and which might better be entitled "a basis for a just society," Gosta Esping-Andersen makes the point that such a society must be based on solidarity. This gives rise to a "set of commitments designed to ensure full social citizenship for all members of society." It is defined as a:

> collective responsibility for the fate of each individual. It directly clashes with the old doctrine that each individual must be responsible for his own happiness and misfortune. Instead, a commitment to social solidarity presupposes that we are all mutually dependent on each other . . . solidarity means that basic human needs have an equal claim on the national wealth and that we are all obligated to pay the necessary costs that such a mutually shared responsibility requires.[100]

It is not, she points out, the level of public spending that characterizes the "welfare state" but the institutionalization of social citizenship. Such a state, she argues, is in its ultimate goal "ultimately incompatible with the dynamics of a capitalist market system" and can only work if its benefits reach all the population.

> As is so painfully evident in contemporary America, middle class support for public services erodes rapidly when their main clientele is poor people.[101]

Most of Europe has adopted some form of universalism. America, which once dreamed of a classless society, alone maintains the means-test for social services. It wants no benefits for the middle classes, one might suggest, because if it did provide them its society would be closer to classless. As Esping-Andersen says, "The toughest obstacle to the achievement of universalism comes from the residual power of the better-off to maintain their privileged position."[102] Nixon vetoed a Day Care bill because some of its benefits would accrue to the middle class; Reagan used the same logic in reducing school lunch subsidies. Logically he should then, of course, have abolished free public schools and make the well-to-do pay individually for police protection.

Reagan insisted, again and again, that his program was compassionate. It was not. Compassion involves some sharing of suffering. What the rich feel, rather, is pity which is grounded in their own sense of superiority. The United States, for the moment, has turned back to the Capitalist-Puritan ethic, ignoring three hundred years of history, and to the "intolerable rule of the Saints." The poor have lost the few rights they had attained and are once again an underclass.

Notes

The Erosion of a Right

[1] This was the general conclusion of my *Decisions About People in Need*, Chapel Hill, 1957.

[2] Baldwin, Joseph, "I Do Believe," *Louisiana Welfare*, 13, (1953): 3.

[3] Ruth Ellen Lindenberg, "Hard to Reach: Client or Casework Agency?" *Social Work*, 3, (1958): 25.

[4] Eileen Younghusband, *Social Work in Britain*, Edinburgh, 1951, p. 90.

[5] Barbara Wooten, "The Image of the Social Worker," *British Journal of Sociology*, 11 (1960): 376.

[6] Ibid., p. 380.

[7] R. B. Perry, *Puritanism and Democracy*, New York, 1944, p. 95.

[8] See, for instance, John J. Stretch, "Existentialism: A Proposed Philosophical Orientation for Social Work," *Social Work*, 12 (1967): 97-102, and Kirk A. Bradford, *Existentialism and Casework*, New York (1969).

[9] Wooten, "The Image of the Social Worker," p. 384.

[10] This is mentioned almost as a matter of course by Werner Boehm, "Casework: A Psychosocial Therapy," *Child Welfare*, 42 (1964): 536.

[11] Alvin Schorr, "The Tendency to Rx," *Social Work*, 7 (1962): 59-66.

[12] David Soyer, "The Right to Fail," *Social Work*, 8 (1963): 72-78.

[13] Felix Biestek, "Problems in Identifying Social Work Values," in *Values in Social Work: a Re-examination*, p. 23.

[14] From a report of a staff-training exercise, Louisiana Department of Public Welfare, 1956.

[15] Martin Eisman, "Social Work's New Role in the Welfare-Class Revolution," *Social Work*, 14, 1 (April 1969): 81.

The Welfare Explosion and Revolt

[16] Kermit Wiltse, describing what was known as the "Contra Costa County Experiment," in "Social Casework Services in the Aid to Dependent Children Program," *Social Service Review*, 28 (1954): 178.

[17] U. S. House of Representatives, Committee on Ways and Means, report accompanying HR 10606, March 18, 1962, p. 3.

[18] Figures from Piven and Cloward, *Regulating the Poor*, pp. 183-187.

[19] Daniel Moynihan, *The Negro Family: the Case for National Action,* U.S. Department of Labor, 1965.

[20] Piven and Cloward, *Regulating the Poor,* p. 198.

[21] Michael Harrington, *The Other America: Poverty in the United States*, New York, 1962.

[22] Ben H. Bagdikian, *In the Midst of Plenty: A New Report on the Poor in America*, Boston, 1964.

[23] It is interesting to note that as late as 1980-1981, there are more articles on homosexuality published in *Social Work* (four in little more than a year) than on any other single subject.

[24] Part of a wall of the assembly room at the Hotel Americana had to be removed to allow delegates to leave one general meeting when the doors were blocked by activists who demanded that the delegates listen to their presentation.

[25] Earl Rash, "A Tale of the Three Wars: (3) What War and Which Poverty?" *Public Interest*, (Spring 1966): 52, quoted by Piven and Cloward, *Regulating the Poor,* p. 272.

[26] According to Piven and Cloward, *Regulating the Poor*, p. 269.

[27] See, *inter alia*, John E. Ehrlich, "Breaking the Dole Barrier: the Lingering Death of the American Welfare System," *Social Work*, 14, 3 (July 1969): 49-55.

[28] Jacobus tenBroek and Richard B. Wilson, "Public Assistance and Social Insurance: A Normative Evaluation," *U.C.L.A. Law Review,* 1 (1954): 266.

[29] Marc Bendick, Jr., "Failure to Enroll in Public Assistance Programs," *Social Work,* 25, (1980): 269-274.

[30] The "Employable Mother" rule was struck down on the grounds, among others, that is was used more frequently to deny benefits to Black mothers and the "employability" was determined merely by the opinion of the welfare worker. The "man in the house" and the "substitute parent" rules were devices to try to prove that a child was not "deprived of parental care and support" if his mother was cohabiting with a man, or even dating him consistently. The court described it as "a transparent fiction," according to Piven and Cloward, *Regulating the Poor*, p. 308-309.

[31] The name of Bennie Parish should be enshrined in the history of social welfare. He was a welfare worker who, in 1962, was dismissed from his job in California for refusing to take part in a midnight raid on welfare clients. Mr. Parish lost his case in court, but in 1970 the principle for which he fought was confirmed. See Piven and Cloward, *Regulating the Poor*, pp. 166 and 311.

[32] For a history of the Food Stamp Program up to 1977, see Jodie T. Allen, "The Food Stamp Program: History and Reform," *Public Welfare,* 35, 3 (Summer 1977): 33-41.

[33] Some services of a "social control" nature, such as protective services for children, would be retained, one imagines, but these were not often discussed in the literature and service delivery at that time.

[34] Quoted from Winifred Bell, "Services for People: An Appraisal," *Social Work*, 15, 3 (July 1970): 9.

[35] For a discussion of the limitations of the "Warehouse" concept, see my "Philosophies of Public Services," *Public Welfare,* 31, 1 (Winter, 1973): 21-25.

[36] Piven and Cloward, Regulating the Poor, pp.291-292.

[37] There are a number of articles on the "indigenous worker," of which perhaps the seminal one is George Brager, "The Indigenous Worker: A New Approach to the Social Work Technician," *Social Work*, 11, 3 (July 1966): 95-101; also Martin Rein and Frank Riessman, "A Strategy for Antipoverty Community Action Programs," *Social Work*, 11, 2 (April 1966): 3-12 for the "expediter" role.

[38] "The Social Worker as Advocate: Champions of Social Victims," *Social Work*, 14, 2 (April 1969): 17.

[39] Robert D. Plotnick, "Progress Against Poverty?", *Social Welfare Forum*, (1976): 104-115.

"Casework is Dead"

[40] Florence Hollis and Mary E. Woods, *Casework, A Psychosocial Therapy*, New York, 1964.

[41] Helen Harris Perlman, *Social Casework: A Problem-Solving Process*, Chicago, 1957.

[42] Anita Faatz, *The Nature of Choice in Casework Process*, Chapel Hill, N.C., 1953.

[43] The first evidence of this would seem to be Henry J. Meyer, Edgar Borgatta and Wyatt Jones, *Girls at Vocational High: An Experiment in Social Work Intervention*, New York, 1965. See Alvin Schorr's review of this in *Social Work,* 10, 3 (July 1965): 112-113.

[44] Joel Fischer, "Is Casework Effective? A Review," *Social Work*, 18, 1 (January 1973): 5-20. The quotation is from a box on p. 9. Dr.Fischer is quick to criticize, on methodological grounds, any study that purports to show that casework had a beneficial effect. In one instance he concluded that, in a certain situation, casework had hastened the deaths of certain aged clients and his methods were in themselves challenged by

other researchers. See Raymond Berger and Irving Piliavin, "The Effect of Casework: A Research Note," *Social Work*, 22 (May 1976): 205-208; Joel Fisher and Walter W. Hudson, "An Effect of Casework? Back to the Drawing Board," ibid., pp.347-349; and Berger and Piliavin's rejoinder, pp.349, 396-397.

[45] Paul Halmos, *The Faith of the Counsellors*, London, 1965, part of Chapter Heading, p.146.

[46] Scott Briar, "The Casework Predicament," *Social Work*, 13, 1 (January 1968): 5-11.

[47] Nathan Cohen, "An Historical Perspective on Social Welfare," *Social Welfare Forum*, (1976): 23.

[48] Ibid., p. 24.

[49] Ibid., p .23.

[50] "Casework is Dead," *Social Casework*, 48 (1967): 22-25; and "Can Casework Work?," Social Service Review, 47 (1968): 435-447.

[51] In an editorial in *Social Work,* of which he was editor, 16, 2 (July 1971): 2.

[52] Harry Specht, "The Deprofessionalization of Social Work," *Social Work*, 17, 2 (March 1972): 3-15.

[53] Martin Rein, "Social Work in Search of a Radical Profession." *Social Work*, 15, 2 (April 1970): 17.

[54] Anita Faatz, *Social Work and the Poverty Program,* Isabelle K. Carter Lecture, May 20, 1965, University of North Carolina, p. 10.

[55] Not to be confused, as the F.B.I. did on several occasions, with Herbert Aptekar, a highly-respected social work writer.

[56] Harry Specht, "Disruptive Tactics," *Social Work,* 14, 2 (April 1969): 14.

[57] Porter R. Lee, "Social Work: Cause and Function," *Proceedings of the National Converence of Social Work*, 1929, pp. 3-20.

[58] Rein, "Social Work in Search of a Radical Profession," p. 28.

[59] Alan D. Wade, as quoted by Mary Gyarfas, "Social Science Technology and Social Work," *Social Service Review*, 43 (1969): 262.

[60] For a short history of private practice in social work, see Estelle Gabriel in the *Encyclopedia of Social Work*, 1977, pp. 1054-1060. In a summary of an article in 1976 (Arnold M. Levin, "Private Practice is-Alive and Well," *Social Work*, 21 (1976): 356-362, private practice is said to help "advance the profession from its anachronistic philanthropic orientation toward a more modern professionalism." (p. 356). See also the *Handbook on the Private Practice of Social Work,* published by the National Association of Social Workers, Washington, 1974.

The "Knowledge Explosion"

Elizabeth L. Salomon, "Humanistic Values and Social Casework," *Social Casework*, 48 (1967): 26-31.

[62] Ibid., p. 28.

[63] The seminal article is perhaps Aaron Rosenblatt's, "The Practitioner's Use and Evaluation of Research," *Social Work*, 13 (1968): 53-59.

[64] Joel Fischer, "The Social Work Revolution," *Social Work*, 26 (1981): 201.

[65] Ibid., p. 205.

[66] Ibid., p. 204.

[67] Ibid., p. 205.

[68] Ronald L. Simons, "Strategies for Exercising Influence," *Social Work*, 27 (1982): 268-274. The editor's caption to this article states that social workers in all practice setting need to exercise influence.

[69] Ronald Paul Salzberger, "Casework and the Client's Right to Self-Determination," *Social Work*, 24 (1979): 40.

[70] Ibid., p. 40.

[71] Walter L. Miller, "Casework and the Medical Model," *Social Work*, 25 (1980): 285

[72] Louise A. Frey and Golda M. Edinburg, "Helping, Manipulation and Magic," *Social Work*, 23 (1978): 91.

[73] F. P. McDonald and Irving Piliavin, "Separation of Services and Income Maintenance: The Worker's Perspective," *Social Work*, 25 (1980): 264-267.

[74] The best known is Daniel Moynihan's *Maximum Feasible Misunderstanding: Community Action in the War on Poverty*, New York, 1969.

[75] See, for instance, Stanley J. Brody, "Maximum Participation of the Poor: Another Holy Grail?" *Social Work*, 15 (1970): 68-75.

Alternatives to the "Welfare Mess"

[76] Karl Hess, "In Pursuit of Wealth, Not Welfare," *Public Welfare*, 39, 1 (Winter 1981): 19-21. See also the accompanying article, Sam Brown's "An Old Idea Whose Time Has Come," Ibid., 13-18.

[77] See Sydney E. Zimbalist, "Comparison of Social Welfare Values: A Semantic Approach," *Social Work*, 23 (1978): 200-201. He contrasts Britain's "longstanding tradition of reciprocal fair play and social justice" with America's "greater emphasis on self-sufficient rugged individualism."

[78] Representative articles are Irwin Garfinkel's "Negative Income Tax and Children's Allowance Programs: A Comparison," *Social Work*, 13 (1968): 33-39; George Hoshino's "Britain's Debate on Universal or Selective Social Services: Lessons for America," *Social Service Review*, 44 (1960): 245-258; George F. Rohrlich's "Guaranteed Minimum Income Proposals and the Unfinished Business of Social Security," *Social Service Review*, 41 (1967): 166-178; and Alvin Schorr's "Alternatives in Income Maintenance," *Social Work*, 11, 3 (July 1966): 22-29.

[79] For descriptions of the Carter program see Irwin Garfinkel, "What's Wrong with Welfare?" *Social Work*, 23 (1978): 185-191; and "A Look at Welfare Reform," statements by Joseph A. Califano, Henry Aaron and Suzanne Woolsey, *Public Welfare*, 335, 3 (Summer 1977): 10-23.

[80] James A Rotherman, "The Carter Budget: Its New Human Resources Initiatives," Ibid., p. 24.

[81] Leonard Goodwin, "Can Welfare Work?" *Public Welfare*, 39, 4 (Fall 1981): 19-25.

[82] Arthur H. Miller, "Will Public Attitudes Defeat Welfare Reform?" *Public Welfare*, 36 (Summer 1978): 52.

[83] Figures from Joseph M. Dukert, "Who is Poor? Who is Truly Needy?" *Public Welfare*, 41, 1 (Winter 1983): 20.

[84] Quoted by Jodie T. Allen, "The Food Stamp Program: Its History and Reform," *Public Welfare*, 35, 3 (Summer 1977): 35.

[85] Senator McGovern quotes a Field Foundation Report to Congress (96th Congress, Subcommittee on Nutrition: "Hunger in America: Ten Years Later") to the effect that although povery continued to exist in the areas the researcher studied, hunger and malnutrition were no longer a problem, due largely to Food Stamps, school lunches and breakfasts and supplemental feeding programs for women, infants and children, "Whose Responsibility is Social Responsibility? An Opposing View," *Public Welfare*, 39, 4 (Fall 1981): 14.

The Conservative Reaction

[86] Robert B. Carleson and Kevin B. Hopkins, "Whose Responsibility is Social Responsibility? The Reagan Rationale," ibid., p. 10

[87] Ibid.

[88] Ibid., pp. 11-12. The quote is from the United State's Chamber of Commerce's fact pamphlet, *The Researchers Destroy Some Welfare Myths*, Washington, 1979.

[89] Ibid., p .15.

[90] Ibid.

[91] Piven and Cloward, *the New Class War,* p. 130.

[92] Carleson and Hopkins, "The Reagan Rationale," p. 8.

[93] "Cheating by the Millions," *Time* (March 8, 1983): 28-33.

[94] Carleson and Hopkins, "The Reagan Rationale," p. 9.

[95] Gilder, *Wealth and Poverty,* p. 68.

[96] Ibid., p. 69.

[97] Ibid., p. 73.

[98] Ibid., p. 68.

[99] Ibid., p. 117.

[100] Gosta Esping-Anderson, "After the Welfare State," originally published in *Working Papers for a New Society,* May/June, 1982, but reprinted in *Public Welfare,* 41, 1 (Winter 1983): 28-30.

[101] Ibid., p. 31.

[102] Ibid.

CHAPTER 6

Foundations Re-Visited: Judeo-Christian Hopes for a Just Society

What Hope for the Future?

Ready to Share?

It does not seem possible that the United States can continue to live in the Eighteenth or Nineteenth centuries for very many years. What will happen to change this, I do not think anyone knows.

It may be simply a revulsion, once what this philosophy entails becomes more apparent. There are forces in the country that recognize man's interdependence and have a feeling for solidarity. There may be a period of euphoria on the part of the middle class, who resent most having to share with the poor. And then a great disillusionment if there should be another and more serious recession or even depression, which would appear to be inevitable in a system that accords to the money-market most of the attributes of Providence. Piven and Cloward, writing in 1981, were optimistic in believing that so many groups would be outraged by the Reagan policies that he would not be re-elected in 1984.[1] He was, of course, by a huge majority. There seems to be little feeling for the poor. Middle-class youths in California are even reported as beating up on street-people, winos, and derelicts because they lower the tone of the community. It does not look as if the United States is ready to share.

There may conceivably be sufficient challenge from developing countries and a consequent falling-off in the American standard of living that Americans are forced to give up the belief that anyone can rely entirely on his or her own efforts to achieve some sort of security. There may be civil unrest, or, if Piven and Cloward are correct in their interpretation of how governments behave, a fear of civil unrest and an attempt on the part of the government to placate it.[2] It is perhaps significant that Reagan's apologists, at a time when civil unrest seemed rather unlikely, found it necessary to insist that:

> no threat of unrest should be permitted to cow a government into transferring income from one group of people to

another when that transfer is not justified by accepted social norms.[3]

The "social norms" assumed here are, of course, defined as those natural rights to one's earnings and not those of a shared responsibility. It may be that nuclear war may render the whole question moot. There will be no rich or poor; only the living (rather few of them) and the dead.

Sooner or Later

If this does not happen, however, it seems reasonable to assume that to when America will follow most of the rest of the industrialized world, capitalist or socialist, in establishing some sort of a guaranteed income and probably some sort of assurance that one can obtain medical care. In general, America has followed Europe in welfare matters, about forty years later. If this pattern is maintained, family allowances, which even George Gilder approves of,[4] are due in the near future, and so is some kind of national health insurance. There will have to be, not "income transfers" which is a loaded phrase suggesting a forced redistribution, but some pooling of effort and common responsibility.

I hope that this will come about peacefully. I think it has a chance to do so, despite the temptations of egoism and the old sin of Pride. I think it may come about when more and more people begin to realize that the world has become so complicated and complex that perfectly ordinary people are finding it almost impossible to manage without help.

One social worker, Loewenstein, has already suggested that in a very few years everybody will need help in at least three areas of his life: how to cope with organizations, such as a hospital, a school board, an insurance system; how to play social roles for which one has not been prepared, such as single parent, retiree, stepparent, hospital patient; and what life-style to adopt. He ends his statement:

> In the emerging post-industrial society these problems will not be those of just a disadvantaged or madjusted minority. Rather, they will be normal problems that each individual will confront in attempting to organize his life and coordinate it within a rapidly changing social environment. Consequently, help with these problems will be routine, necessary, and universal.[5]

144

It might be added that these problems will be almost insoluble without the material means to accomplish them, and that they are, to a large extent, the reason why material means are lacking.

What Would It Include?

It would be tempting, if perhaps a little presumptuous, to try to envisage what anyone, poor or not, could expect of a just, sharing society. There have been in social work literature a number of attempts to describe a "right" relationship between individuals and society, generally under the rubric of enunciating social work values.[6] Such statements tend to be, however, rather more philosophical than specific. Apart from a reasonable standard of living, a decent place to live, and access to medical care and education, perhaps the most useful formulation is one offered by Morton I. Teicher. Based on the general statement that each individual has dignity and worth, he believes that each individual ought:

- to take part in making the decisions that affect him or her
- to share fairly in the control of goods and services
- to receive respect and considerate treatment (from, it is presumed, officials and others in authority)
- to have a full and free access to the information needed for rational behavior
- to be free to develop his or her own capacity and talents
- to enjoy the benefits of our knowledge of health and well-being
- to have opportunities to experience affection and companionship.[7]

The last may be a little difficult to ensure, but the others are surely all attainable, even for the poor.

The Judeo-Christian Tradition

A Return

If this transformation takes place peacefully, as everyone hopes that it will, what it will in effect entail is a return to the Judeo-Christian tradition.

This statement may seem extraordinary after we have explored at length the negative effects of Christian dogma on the care of the poor, and it could be held that Capitalist-Puritan ideology was in fact in the Christian, if not the Jewish, tradition. Yet this corrupted world view is at best a little more than three centuries old and can be shown in many ways to contradict the essential teaching of the two religions.

There is, in fact, a world view, Biblical in its origin, that stands apart from and yet behind both Capitalist-Puritan and Humanist-Positivist-Utopian thought and from which both could be said to be deviations. It does not depend, let us be clear, on individual texts taken out of context, but on the whole sweep of the story and has been nurtured through the ages by theologians from Origen to Buber, Berdyaev, and Tillich and inumerable others. It may not even be recognized by many as specifically Judeo-Christian, and yet it is so.

Foundations

The essential tenets of this world view, expressed largely in secular terms, but with some reference to their origin, might be expressed as follows:

1. Humans are creatures, not autonomous beings, with responsibilities to each other (and, religiously, to their Creator). It is when humans forget this fact, and rely on their own wisdom, that they generally get into trouble, tend to pervert their institutions, and end up by a self-appointed few trying to control the others.

2. Humans are neither totally good nor bad, but this does not mean that they are basically amoral.[8] They are very fallible but can also transcend themselves at times. (This, in religious thinking, is ascribed to Grace.) There also are not "good" and "bad" people but a mixture of goodness and badness in everyone, as well as wisdom and foolishness, which precludes those who claim to be good or wise from blaming or prescribing for those they consider bad or foolish. (In religious terms this may be expressed as that "there is now no distinction, since all have fallen short of the glory of God," Romans 3:22).

3. Human beings have been endowed with the faculty of choice, necessary to their development as fully sentient beings, but they also cannot escape the consequences of their choice. Their choices as to how they will respond to circumstances cannot be made for them by any other person.

4. Justice requires that humans share to some extent in the good things of life. This includes full citizenship and access to opportunities to reach one's potential. Humans are interdependent. When any one hurts, all suffer.[9] Personal wealth, whether earned or inherited, is entrusted to one and carries responsibility for the

146

general good. One does not have an absolute right to manage it as one wishes.

5. The goal, in this life at least, is a state of active and involved well-being in which one can experience the two ultimate human emotions, love and joy. These cannot be sought for their own sake, but are the result of serving others or creating worthwhile things.[10] (In religious thinking, this state includes life after death and communion with God. It is what is meant by Salvation.)

6. The essential motivator, both personal and societal, is love. In religious thinking, this begins with God's love for His creatures but it is also true of their relationship with each other. Love is the source of good behavior, rather than good behavior earning love. Love is also the eventual victor. Force may accomplish immediate ends, but in the long run is self-defeating. Only love produces permanent results.[11]

7. All human beings are of infinite worth, irrespective of their behavior. (In religious terms they are children of God and those for whom Christ died.) Every one of them is worthy of our consideration, however wayward they may seem.

Hope

This, I would maintain, is the true Judeo-Christian tradition, stripped of many accretions and not a few perversions, many of which are basically self-seeking, assuring benefits to oneself and denying them to others. In relation to the care of the poor, there is hope that this view of humankind and society may be more prevalent in the future. Not only is there added interest among many scientists and other humanists in the insights of religion but an influx of young Christians into the social work profession, to whom the care of the poor is largely entrusted. One third of all undergraduate social work programs are now in church-related colleges and universities.

It will matter, of course, tremendously what kind of Christianity these new workers profess.

If they are Christians of Grace,[12] those who fully understand the tradition and see themselves as God's clients, the recipients of His Love, there is real reason to hope.

If they are primarily Christians of Law, those who think salvation has only been offered to those who keep all the rules and believe the right things, we will continue to have a group in society especially conforming and submissive in order to survive.

And if they should be Christians of Morality, those who imagine themselves to be God's lieutenants to reform the world, we will again have an underclass, despised by the well-to-do, and once again writhing under the "intolerable rule of the saints."

Notes

What Hopes for the Future?

[1] Piven and Cloward, *The New Class War,* pp .139-143.

[2] This is the contention of Piven and Cloward's former book, *Regulating the Poor,* which was published in 1971. In 1981 they modified this view some, not in relation to the past but to the future. See *The New Class War,* pp. x-xi.

[3] Carleson and Hopkins, "The Reagan Rationale," p. 16.

[4] Gilder, *Wealth and Poverty,* p. 126-127.

[5] Edward R. Loewenstein, "Social Work in a Post Industrial Society," *Social Work,* 33, 6 (November 1973): 47.

[6] Notably "The Working Definition of Social Work Practice," as presented by Harriet Bartlett, "Towards Clarification and Improvement of Social Work Practice," *Social Work,* 3, 2 (April 1958): 3-9; William E. Gordon, "A Critique of the Working Definition," ibid., 8, 4 (October 1962): 3-13; and Felix P. Biestek, "Problems in Identifying Social Work Values," in *Values in Social Work: A Re-Examination,* 1965, pp. 31-39.

[7] Morton I. Teicher, "Conclusion and Summary," *In Values in Social Work,* pp. 100-109.

The Judeo-Christian Tradition

[8] Bisno, in his *Philosophy of Social Work,* holds as one of his basic principles that "man is amoral and asocial at birth," p. 16.

[9] Eugene Debs is quoted as saying, "While there is a man in prison, I am not free."

[10] There are a number of things which cannot be found by looking for them. these include happiness, job satisfaction, self-fulfilment, and relationship with others. Aristotle said that happiness could not be sought. It was the result of a "virtuous" (actively involved) life. C. S. Lewis was "surprised by joy" and Jesus said that he who would find his life would lose it.

[11] "Love" is a difficult word. What is meant here is *Agape,* the best description of which is found in I Corinthians 13.

[12] For further discussion of the terms used here, see my *The Client's Religion and Your Own Beliefs in the Helping Process: A Guide for Believers and Non-Believers,* Chapel Hill, N.C., now published by the National Foundation for Services to Children, Chino, CA.

BIBLIOGRAPHY

I
SOURCE BOOKS CONTAINING, REPRODUCING OR EXCERPTING AT LENGTH MORE THAN ONE ARTICLE

Barnes, H. E., Howard and Frances Bennet Becker, *Contemporary Social Theory,* New York, 1940.

Breckenridge, Sophonisba, ed., *Public Welfare Administration in the United States: Select Documents,* Chicago, 1927.

de Schweinitz, Karl, *England's Road to Social Security,* Philadelphia, 1943.

Encyclopedia of the Social Sciences, New York, 1930-1935.

Encyclopedia of Social Work, Seventeenth Issue, 1977.

Goodwin, Michael, ed., *Nineteenth Century Opinion,* London, 1951.

Haber, W. and W. J. Cohen, eds., *Readings in Social Security,* New York, 1948.

Kasius, Cora, ed., *Principles and Techniques in Social Case Work: Selected Articles, 1940-50,* New York, 1950.

Lowry, Fern, ed., *Readings in Social Case Work,* 1920-1938.

Lubbock, Gertrude, *Some Poor Law Questions,* London, 1895.

National Association of Social Workers, *Values in Social Work: a Re-examination,* New York, 1965.

National Conference of Social Work, *Selected Papers in Casework,* 1952.

Pumphrey, Ralph E. and Muriel W., *The Heritage of American Social Work,* New York and London, 1961.

Reed, John, *Ten Days that Shook the World,* England, 1926.

Social Work as Human Relations: Anniversary Papers of the New York School of Social Work and the Community Service Society of New York, New York, 1949.

II
OTHER BOOKS AND PAMPHLETS

Abbott, Edith, *Public Assistance: American Principles and Policies,* Chicago, 1940.

Addams, Jane, *Philanthropy and Social Process,* New York, 1893.

Addams, Jane, *Twenty Years at Hull House,* New York, 1910.

Aptekar, Herbert, *The Dynamics of Casework and Counselling,* Boston, 1955.

Bagdikian, Ben H, *In the Midst of Plenty: A New Report on the Poor in America*, Boston, 1964.

Barry, F. R., *The Relevance of Christianity*, London, 1931.

Berdyaev, Nicolai, *Slavery and Freedom*, trans. by R. M. French, New York, 1944.

Biestek, Felix P. and Clyde C. Gehrig, *Client Self-Determination in Social Work: A Fifty-Year History*, Chicago, 1978.

Borgatta, Edward and Wyatt Jones, *Girls at Vocational High: An Experiment in Social Work Intervention*, New York, 1965.

Bradford, Kirk A., *Existentialism and Casework*, New York, 1969.

Brandt, Lillian, *How Much Shall I Give?* New York, 1921.

Brown, Norman O, *Life Against Death.* New York, 1959.

Buber, Martin, *I and Thou*, trans. by Ronald Gregor Smith, London, 1937.

Butler, Samuel, *Erewhon*, London, 1903.

Butler, Samuel, *The Way of All Flesh*, London, 1903.

Butterfield, Herbert, *Christianity and History*, New York, 1949.

Carkhuff, Robert R., *Helping and Human Relations*, New York, 1969.

Coghill, Nevill, *Visions from Piers Plowman*, London, 1949.

Davis, Allen F., *Spearheads for Reform: the Social Settlements and the Progressive Movement, 1890-1914*, New York, 1967.

Davis, Annie Lee, *Children Living in Their Own Homes*, Washington, 1953.

Dawson, Christopher, *Mediaeval Religion and Other Essays*, London, 1934.

de Schweinitz, Karl, *People and Process in Social Security*, Washington, 1948.

de Schweinitz, Karl and Elizabeth, *The Content of the Public Assistance Job*, New York, n.d.

Devine, Edward, *The Principles of Relief*, New York, 1904.

Douglas, Paul, *Social Security in the United States*, New York, 1936.

Eden, Sir Frederick, *The State of the Poor: Or An History of the Labouring Classes, from the Conquest to the Present Period*, London, 1797.

Faatz, Anita, *The Nature of Choice in Casework Process*, Chapel Hill, N.C., 1953.

Faatz, Anita, *Social Work and the Poverty Program*, Isabelle K. Carter Lecture, University of North Carolina, 1965.

Fromm, Erich, *Man for Himself: An Enquiry into the Psychology of Ethics*, New York, 1947.

Fromm, Erich, *The Art of Loving,* New York, 1956.

Gilder, George, *Wealth and Poverty*, New York, 1982.

Hamilton, Gordon, *The Theory and Practice of Social Casework*, New York, 1940.

Harrington, Michael, *The Other America: Poverty in the United States*, New York, 1962.

Hollis, E. V. and A. L. Taylor, *Social Work Education in the United States*, New York, 1951.

Hollis, Florence, *Social Casework in Practice: Six Case Studies*, New York, 1939.

Hollis, Florence and Mary E. Woods, *Casework, a Psychosocial Therapy*. New York, 1964.

Hubbard, G. E., *The Old Book of Wye*, Derby, 1951.

Kasius, Cora, ed., *A Comparison of Diagnostic and Functional Casework Concepts*, New York, 1950.

Keith-Lucas, Alan, *Decisions About People in Need*, Chapel Hill, N.C., 1957.

Keith-Lucas, Alan, *Giving and Taking Help*, Chapel Hill, N.C., 1972.

Keith-Lucas, Alan, *The Client's Religion and Your Own Beliefs in the Helping Process*, Chapel Hill, N.C., 1983.

Knights, L. C., *How Many Chairmen Had Lady Macbeth?* Cambridge, 1931.

Konopka, Gisela, *Edward C. Lindeman and Social Work Philosophy*, Minneapolis, 1958.

Kurtz, Russell, ed., *The Public Assistance Worker*, New York, 1938.

Kutzik, Alfred J., *Social Work and Jewish Values*, Washington, 1959.

Lallemand, Leon, *Histoire de la Charité*, Paris, 1902-06.

Lasswell, H. D., *Psychopathology and Politics*, New York, 1930.

Lippmann, Walter, *Public Opinion*, New York, 1922.

Loch, G. S., *Charity and Social Life*, London, 1910.

Lou, Herbert H., *Juvenile Courts in the United States*, Chapel Hill, N.C., 1927.

Marcus, Grace, *The Nature of Service in Public Assistance Administration*, Washington, 1947.

Masterman, N., ed., *Chalmers on Charity: A Selection of Passages and Scenes to Illustrate the Social Teaching and Practical Work of Thomas Chalmers, D.D.*, Westminster, 1900.

Mayhew, Henry, *London Labour and the London Poor*, London, 1861-1862.

McCormick, Mary J., *Diagnostic Casework in the Thomistic Pattern*, New York, 1954.

McDermott, F. E., ed., *Self-Determination in Social Work*, London, 1975.

Merriam, Lewis, *Relief and Social Security*, Washington, 1946.

Miles, A. P., *American Social Work Theory: A Critique and a Proposal*, New York, 1954.

Moynihan, Daniel, *The Negro Family: the Case for National Action*, New York, 1969.

Moynihan, Daniel, *Maximum Feasible Misunderstanding: Community Action in the War on Poverty*, New York, 1969.

Niebuhr, H. Richard, *The Social Sources of Denominationalism*, New York, 1929.

Niebuhr, Reinold, *The Contribution of Religion to Social Work*, New York, 1932.

Perlman, Helen Harris, *Social Casework: A Problem-Solving Process*, Chicago, 1957.

Perry, R. B., *Puritanism and Democracy*, New York 1944.

Piven, Frances Fox and Richard A. Cloward, *Regulating the Poor*, New York, 1971.

Piven, Frances Fox and Richard A. Cloward, *The New Class War*, New York, 1981.

Pray, Kenneth L. M., *Social Work in a Revolutionary Age and Other Papers*, Philadelphia, 1948.

Quennel, Peter, ed., *Mayhew's London*, 1951.

Reckitt, Maurice B., *Religion in Social Action*, London, 1937.

Reynolds, Bertha, *Re-Thinking Social Case Work*, San Diego, 1936.

Reynolds, Bertha, *Social Work and Social Living*, New York, 1951.

Richmond, Mary, *Social Diagnosis*, New York, 1917.

Richmond, Mary, *What is Social Case Work?*, New York, 1922.

Richmond, Mary, *The Long View*, New York, 1930.

Robertson, H. M., *The Rise of Economic Individualism*, Cambridge, 1933.

Robinson, Virginia, *A Changing Psychology in Social Work*, Chapel Hill, N.C., 1930.

Rodgers, Betsy, *The Cloak of Charity*, London, 1949.

Sayers, Dorothy, *The Other Six Deadly Sins*, London, 1943.

Skinner, B. F., *Beyond Freedom and Dignity*, Harmondsworth, England, 1973.

Smith, A. Delafield, *The Right to Life*, Chapel Hill, N.C., 1955.

Social Security Board, *Social Security in America*, 1937.

Socialt Tidskrift, *Social Denmark*, Copenhagen, 1947.

Tawney, R. H., *Religion and the Rise of Capitalism*, London, 1926.

Tillyard, E. M. W., *The Elizabethan World View*, London, 1945.

Titmuss, Richard M., *Essays on the Welfare State*, London, 1958.

Towle, Charlotte, *Common Human Needs*, Washington, 1945.

Trevelyan, G. M., *History of England*, London, 1945.

Trilling, Lionel, *Freud and the Crisis of Our Culture*, Boston, 1935.

Trilling, Lionel, *The Liberal Imagination*, New York, 1950.

Troeltsch, Ernest, *The Social Teaching of the Christian Churches*, trans. by Olive Wyon, New York, 1931.

Tuchman, Barbara, *The Proud Tower*, New York, 1966.

Uhlhorn, G., *Christian Charity in the Ancient Church*, Edinburgh, 1883.

United States Department of Health, Education and Welfare, *Standards for Juvenile and Family Courts*, Washington, 1966.

Virtue, Maxine Board, *Study of the Basic Structure of Children's Services in Michigan*, Ann Arbor, 1953.

Voegelin, Erich, *The New Science of Politics*, Chicago, 1952.

Weber, Max, *The Protestant Ethic and the Spirit of Capitalism*, trans. by Talcott Parsons, London, 1930.

Wettenbaker, Thomas Jefferson, *The Puritan Oligarchy*, New York, 1947.

Young, A. F. and E. T. Ashton, *British Social Work in the Nineteenth Century*, New York, 1956.

Young, Pauline V., *Social Treatment in Probation and Delinquency*, New York, 1952.

Younghusband, Eileen, *Social Work in Britain*, Edinburgh, 1951.

III
ARTICLES AND REPORTS
(those marked * are found in the Sources Book cited. See I above.)

Addams, Jane, "The Subtle Problems in Charity," 1899, in *Heritage*.*

Allen, Jodie T., "The Food Stamp Program: Its History and Reform," *Public Welfare*, 35 (1977).

All-Russian Central Executive Committee of the Soviets of Workers' and Soldiers' Deputies (Tsay-ee-kah), *"Nakaz" to Skobeliev*, in *Ten Days*.*

Altmeyer, Arthur J., "Ten Years of Social Security," in *Readings in Social Security*.*

Associated Charities of Boston, Fourth Annual Report, 1883, in *Heritage*.*

Association for the Improvement of the Condition of the Poor, "Cofidential Instructions to the Visitors of the AICP," 1885, in *Heritage*.

Baldwin, Joseph, "I Do Believe," *Louisiana Welfare*, 13 (1953).

Barnett, Samuel A., "Distress in East London," 1886, in *Nineteenth Century*.*

Bartlett, Harriet, "Towards Clarification and Improvement of Social Work Practice," *Social Work*, 3, 2 (1958): 3-10.

Bell, Winifred, "Services for People: An Appraisal," *Social Work*, 15. 3 (1970): 5-12.

Bendick, Marc, Jr., "Failure to Enrol in Public Assistance Programs," *Social Work*, 25, 4 (1980): 268-274.

Berger, Raymond and Irving Piliavin, "The Effect of Casework: A Research Note," *Social Work*, 21, 5 (1976): 349.

Bernstein, Saul, "Self-Determination, King or Citizen in the Realm of Values?" *Social Work*, 5, 1 (1960): 3-8.

Biestek, Felix P., "The Principle of Client Self-Determination," *Social Casework*, 23 (1951).

Biestek, Felix P., "Basic Values in Social Work," in *Values*,* 1965.

Biestek, Felix P., "Problems in Identifying Social Work Values," in *Values*,* 1965.

Blackley, William Lewery, "National Insurance: A Cheap, Practical Means of Abolishing Poor Rates," 1878, in *Heritage*.*

Boehm, Werner, "Casework: A Psychosocial Therapy," *Child Welfare*, 43, 10 (1964): 535-538.

Bonaparte, Charles J., "The Ethics of Organized Charity," 1893, in *Heritage*.*

Bowers, Swithun, "Social Work and Human Problems," *Social Casework*, 35 (1954).

Brace, Charles Loring, "Short Sermons to New Boys," 1866, excerpted in *Heritage*.*

Brager, George, "The Indigenous Worker: A New Approach to the Social Work Technician," *Social Work*, 10 (1965): 33-40.

Briar, Scott, "The Casework Predicament," *Social Work*, 13,1 (1968): 5-11.

Brody, Stanley J., "Maximum Participation of the Poor: Another Holy Grail?" *Social Work*, 15, 1 (1970): 68-75.

Brown, Sam, "An Old Idea Whose Time Has Come," *Public Welfare*, 39, 1 (1981): 13-18.*

Bury, W., "Poor Law Progress and Reform," 1889, in *Some Poor Law Questions*.*

Califano, Joseph, et al., "A Look at Welfare Reform," *Public Welfare*, 35, 3 (1977): 12.

Cannon, Mary Antoinette, "Guiding Motives in Social Work," in *New Directions*,* (1954).

Carleson, Robert B. and Kevin B. Hopkins, "Whose Responsibility is Social Responsibility: the Reagan Rationale," *Public Welfare*, 39, 4 (1981), 8.

Carter, Isabelle, Reviews of Gordon Hamilton, *The Theory and Practice of Social Case Work* and Florence Hollis, *Social Case Work in Practice: Six Case Studies*, in *Social Forces*, 19 (1940).

Cohen, Nathan, "An Historical Perspective on Social Welfare," *Social Welfare Forum*, 1976.

Danstedt, Rudolph, "A Possibility for Social Rehabilitation," *Public Welfare*, 8 (1952).

Davis, Allen F., "Settlements: History," *Encyclopedia of Social Work,* * 1977.

de Schweinitz, Karl and Elizabeth, "The Place of Authority in the Protective Function of the Public Welfare Agency," *Child Welfare League Bulletin*, 25, 9 (September 1946) and *Child Welfare*, 43 (1964).

Dougherty, George V., "The Moral Basis of Social Order According to S. Thomas," *Philosophical Studies of the Catholic University of America*, 63 (1941).

Dukert, Joseph M., "Who Is Poor? Who Is Truly Needy?" *Public Welfare*, 41 (1983).

Ehrlich, John E., "Breaking the Dole Barrier: the Lingering Death of the American Welfare System," *Social Work*, 14, 3 (1969): 49-57.

Eisman, Martin., "Social Work's New Role in the Welfare-Class Revolution," *Social Work*, 14, 2 (1969): 80-86.

Esping-Andersen, Gosta, "After the Welfare State," *Public Welfare*, 41, 1 (1983).

Federal Security Agency, *Money Payments to Recipients of Old Age Assistance, Aid to Dependent Children and Aid to the Blind*, Washington, 1944.

Fischer, Joel, "Is Casework Effective? A Review," *Social Work*, 18, 1 (1973): 5-21.

Fischer, Joel, and Walter W. Hudson, "An Effect of Casework: Back to the Drawing Board," *Social Work*, 21,5 (1976): 347-348.

Fischer, Joel, "The Social Work Revolution," *Social Work*, 26,3 (1981): 199-209.

Freeman, Mrs. H. F., "Lend a Hand," 1890, in *Heritage.* *

Frey, A. Louise and Golda M. Edinburg, "Helping, Manipulation and Magic," *Social Work*, 23, 2 (1978): 88-92.

Gabriel, Estelle, "Private Practice in Social Work," *Encyclopedia of Social Work,* * 1977.

Gandelman, Josephine, "Care of Children in Their Own Homes," *Roundup* (Proceedings of the Southwest Regional Conference, American Public Welfare Association, Fort Worth, Texas, 1949).

Garfinkel, Irwin, "Negative Income Tax and Children's Allowance Programs: A Comparison," *Social Work*, 13,4 (1968): 33-39.

George, Henry, "The Reduction to Iniquity," 1884, in *Nineteenth Century*.*

Goodwin, Leonard, "Can Workfare Work?" *Public Welfare*, 36,2 (1978): 39-45.

Gordon, William E, "A Critique of the Working Definition," *Social Work*, 7,4 (1962): 3-13.

Greg, W. R., "A Grave Perplexity Before Us," 1879, in *Nineteenth Century*.*

Griscome, John H. *The Sanitary Condition of the Laboring Population of New York*, 1845, excerpted in *Heritage*.*

Gurteen, Rev. S. Humphreys, *A Handbook of Charity Organization*, excerpted in *Heritage*.*

Gyarfus, Mary, "Social Science Technology and Social Work," *Social Service Review*, 43,3 (1969): 257-274.

Hamilton, Gordon, "Basic Concepts in Social Work," in *Readings in Social Case Work*,* (1939).

Hamilton, Gordon, "The Status of Social Casework Today," in *Readings in Social Casework*,* (1939).

Hamilton, Gordon, "The Underlying Philosophy of Social Casework," 1941, in *Principles and Techniques*.*

Hamilton, Gordon, "Helping People: the Growth of a Profession," 1949, in *Social Work as Human Relations*.*

Hamilton, Gordon, "The Role of Social Casework in Social Policy," *Selected Papers in Casework*, National Conference of Social Work, 1952.

Harding, D. W., Review of Phillip Reiff, T*he Mind of a Moralist, Spectator*, London, February 12, 1960.

Hess, Karl, "In Pursuit of Wealth, not Welfare," *Public Welfare*, 39,1 (1981): 19-22.

Hill, Octavia, Evidence before the Royal Commission on the Aged Poor, 1895, in *Some Relief Questions*.*

Hoey, Jane, "The Significance of the Money Payments in Public Assistance," *Social Security Bulletin*, 7, (1944).

Hoshino, George, "Britain's Debate on Universal or Selective Social Services: Lessons for America," *Social Service Review*, 43, 3 (1969): 245-258.

Hutchinson, Dorothy, "Re-examination of some Aspects of Case Work Practice in Adoption," *Child Welfare League of America Bulletin*, 25 (1946).

Illinois, State of, *Eighth Annual Report of the State Commission of Public Charities*, 1884, in *Breckinridge.**

Kahn, Dorothy, "Conserving Human Values in Public Welfare Programs," *Proceedings of the National Conference of Social Work*, 1939.

Keith-Lucas, Alan, "The Political Theory Implicit in Social Casework Theory," *American Political Science Review*, 67 (1953).

Keith-Lucas, Alan, "A Critique of the Principle of Client Self-Determination," *Social Work*, 8, 3 (1963): 66-72.

Keith-Lucas, Alan, ""Does Welfare Cause Immorality?" *Presbyterian Survey*, 55, 9 (September 1965).

Keith-Lucas, Alan, "Philosophies of Public Service, *Public Welfare*", 31, 1 (Winter 1973): 21-24.

Keith-Lucas, B., "A Local Act for Social Insurance in the Eighteenth Century," *Cambridge Law Journal*, 11 (1952).

Klein, Phillip, "Social Work," *Encyclopedia of the Social Sciences.** (1930-1935).

Klein, Philip, "The Social theory of Professional Social Work," 1940, in *Contemporary Social Theory.**

Kraus, Hertha M. "The Role of Social Case Work in American Social Work," in *Principles** (1950).

Lane, Lionel. "The 'Aggressive' Approach in Preventive Casework with Children's Problems", *Social Casework*, 33 (1952).

League of Local Welfare Executives, *The Good Old Days*, Richmond, Va., 1950.

Lee, Porter R., "Social Work: Cause and Function," *Proceedings of the National Conference of Social Work*, 1929.

Lehrman, Louis J., "The Logic of Diagnosis," *Social Casework*, 35 (1953).

Leiby, James, "Social Welfare: History of Basic Ideas," *Encyclopedia of Social Work,** 1977.

Levin, Arnold M., "Private Practice is Alive and Well," *Social Work*, 21, 5 (1976): 356-362.

Levinson, Perry and Jeffrey Schiller, "A Role Analysis of the Indigenous Nonprofessional," *Social Work*, 11, 3 (1966): 95-101.

Lewis, Verl, "Charity Organization Society," *Encyclopedia of Social Work,** 1977.

Lindenberg, Ruth Ellen, "Hard to Reach: Client or Casework Agency?" *Social Work*, 3, 4 (1958): 23-29.

Lockwood, Allison, "The Street People of London," *British Heritage*, 3 (1982).

Loewenstein, Edward P., "Social Work in a Post-Industrial Society," *Social Work*, 18, 6 (1973): 40-47.

Lowell, Josephine Shaw, "The Economic and Moral Effects of Outdoor Relief," in *Heritage*.*

Lunatcharsky, A. V., "On Popular Education," 1917, in *Ten Days*.*

McDonald, F. P. and Irving Piliavin, "Separation of Services and Income Maintenance: the Worker's Perspective," *Social Work*, 25,4 (1980): 264-267.

Miller, Arthur H., "Will Public Attitudes Defeat Welfare Reform?" *Public Welfare* 36 (1978).

Miller, Walter L., "Casework and the Medical Model," *Social Work*, 25,4 (1980): 281-285.

National Association of Social Workers, "The Social Worker as Advocate: Champions of Social Victims," *Social Work*, 14, 2 (1969): 16-22.

National Association of Social Workers, *Handbook of the Private Practice of Social Work*, Washington, 1974.

Newman, Edward and Jerry Turem, '"The Crisis of Accountability," *Social Work*, 19, 1 (1974): 5-6.

Notes and Comments by the Editor, "Casework Labeled Undemocratic," *Social Service Review*, 28,2 (1954): 1-2.

Overton, Alice, "Serving Families Who 'Don't Want Help'," *Social Casework*, 34 (1953).

Paine, Robert Treat, "Pauperism in Great Cities: Its Four Chief Causes," 1893, in *Heritage*.*

Perlman, Helen Harris, "Self-Determination: Reality or Illusion?" *Social Service Review*, 39,4 (1965): 410-421.

Perlman, Helen Harris, "Casework is Dead," *Social Casework*, 48 (1967).

Perlman, Helen Harris, "Can Casework Work?" *Social Service Review*, 42, 4 (1968): 435-447.

Plotnick, Robert D., "Progress Against Poverty?" *Social Welfare Forum*, 1976.

Quincy, Josiah, *Report of the Poor Law of Massachusetts, 1821*, in *Breckinridge*.*

Regensburg, Jeanette, "Reaching Children Before the Crisis Comes," *Social Casework*, 34 (1954).

Rein, Martin, "Social Work in Search of a Radical Profession," *Social Work*, 17,2 (1970): 13-28.

Rein, Martin and Frank Riessman, "A Strategy for Antipoverty Community Action Programs," *Social Work*, 11, 2 (1966): 3-12.

Report to the President of the Committee on Economic Security, Washington, 1935.

Richmond, Mary, "The Need for a Training School in Applied Philanthropy," 1897, in *Heritage*.*

Riggs, Frieda, "Individualizing Employment Planning in Aid to Dependent Children Families," *The Family*, 23 (1942): 297-300.

Rohrlich, George F., "Guaranteed Minimum Income Proposals and the Unfinished Business of Social Security," *Social Service Review*, 41, 2 (1967): 166-178.

Rosenblatt, Aaron, "The Practitioner's Use and Evaluation of Research," *Social Work*, 13, 1 (1968): 53-59.

Rotherman, James A., "The Carter Budget: Its New Human Resources Initiatives," *Public Welfare*, 25, 3 (1977): 24-32.

Salamon, Elizabeth L., "Humanistic Values and Social Casework," *Social Casework*, 48 (1967).

Salzberger, Ronald Paul, "Casework and the Client's Right to Self-Determination," *Social Work*, 24, 5 (1979): 398-400.

Schorr, Alvin, "The Tendency to Rx," *Social Work*, 7,1 (1962): 59-66.

Schorr, Alvin, Review of Edgar Borgatta and Wyatt Jones, *Girls at Vocational High, Social Work*, 10, 3 (1965): 112-113.

Schorr, Alvin, "Alternatives to Income Maintenance," *Social Work*, 11, 1 (1966):59-66.

Simons, Ronald L., "Strategies for Exercising Influence," *Social Work*, 27,3 (1982): 268-274.

Smalley, Ruth, "The Relation of the Social Welfare Process to the Purpose of a Public Assistance Program," paper given to the New York State Conference on Social Welfare, 1948.

Smith. A. Delafield, "Community Prerogative and the Legal Rights and Freedom of the Individual," *Social Security Bulletin*, 9 (1946).

Smylie, James H., "Gilder, Gilt and the Needle's Eye," *Presbyterian Outlook*, 164, 4 (April 25, 1982).

Soyer, David, "The Right to Fail," *Social Work*, 8, 3 (1963): 72-78.

Specht, Harry, "Disruptive Tactics," *Social Work*, 14, 2 (1969): 5-15.

Specht, Harry, "The Deprofessionalization of Social Work," *Social Work*, 17, 2 (1972): 3-15.

Steininger, F. H., "Desertion and the A.D.C. Program," *Public Welfare*, 5 (1947).

Stephan, Caroline Emilia, "Receiving Strangers," 1879, in *Nineteenth Century*.*

Stretch, John J., "Existentialism: A Proposed Philosphical Orientation for Social Work," *Social Work*, 12, 4 (1967): 97-102.

Stroup, Herbert H., "The Minister and the Thomistic Social Worker," *Iliff Review*, 17 (1960).

Studt, Elliot, "An Outline for Study of Social Authority Factors in Casework," *Social Casework*, 35, 6 (1954): 231-238.

Swander, Constance M, "A Study of Services Needed in a Public Assistance Program," *Public Welfare*, 5 (1947).

Taylor, Robert E., "The Social Control Function in Social Work," *Social Casework*, 39, 1 (1958): 17-21.

Teicher, Morton I., "Summary and Conclusion," in *Values*,* 1965.

tenBroek, Jacobus and Richard B. Wilson,"Public Assistance and Social Insurance: A Normative Evaluation," *U.C.L.A. Law Review*, 1 (1954).

Thompson, R. E., *Manual for Visitors Among the Poor*, 1879, in *Heritage*.*

United States House of Representatives, *Hearings Before a Subcommittee on Ways and Means*, 1954.

United States House of Representatives, Report Accompanying HR 10606, March 18, 1962.

Warner, Amos G. "Notes on the Statistical Determination of the Causes of Poverty," 1889, in *Heritage*.*

Warner, Amos G., "The Causes of Poverty Further Considered," 1894, in *Heritage*.*

Waelder, Robert, "The Scientific Approach to Casework with Special Emphasis on Psychoanalysis," in *Principles and Techniques* (1950).

Wiltse, Kermit, "Social Casework Services in the Aid to Dependent Children Program," *Social Service Review*, 38 (1954).

Witte, Ernest, "Who Speaks Now for the Child in Public Assistance?" *Child Welfare*, 33, 3 (March 1954).

Woods, Robert A., "University Settlements as Laboratories of Social Science, 1893," in *Heritage*.*

Woodward, Marion, Letter published in *Social Service Review*, 18 (1944).

Wooten, Barbara, "The Image of the Social Worker," *British Journal of Sociology*, 11 (1960).

Zimbalist, Sydney E., "Comparison of Social Welfare Values: A Semantic Approach," *Social Work*, 23, 3 (1978): 198-202.

IV
HISTORIC DOCUMENTS
(in Chronological Order)

Holy Bible, The, c. 1000 B.C.-180 A.D.

Shepherd of Hermas, The, c. 140 A.D.

Clement of Alexandria, C. 150-c.213, *Quis Dives Salvatur?*

Constitutions of the Apostles, (pseudepigraph), Second Century.

Ignatius, 3rd Century, *Epistle to Polycarp*.

Ambrose, 340-390, *De Officio Ministrorum*.

John of Antioch (Chrysostom), 347-407, *Seventeenth Homily on Second Corinthians*.

John of Antioch (Chrysostom), *Fourteenth Homily on the Book of Romans*.

John of Antioch (Chrysostum), *Fourth Homily on Lazarus*.

Augustine of Hippo, 354-430, *De Civitate Dei*.

Aquinas, Thomas, 1224-1274, *Summa Theologica*.

Aquinas, Thomas, *De Regemine Principum*.

Langland, William, *The Vision of William about Piers the Plowman and Visions of the Same about Do-Well, Do-Better and Do-Best*, cc. 1380.

Knox, John, *The Buke of Discipline*, 1560.

More, Sir Thomas, *Utopia*, 1516.

Vives, Juan Luis, *De Subventione Pauperum,* 1531.

Vives, Juan Luis, *Forma de Subventione Pauperum*, 1535.

Westminster Confession of Faith, 1646.

Westminster Larger Catechism, 1646.

Leo XIII, *Rerum Novarum,* 1891.

Pius XI, *Quadragesimo Anno*, 1931.

INDEX

A
Abbot, Edith and Grace 82
Addams, Jane 67, 68, 69, 70, 71, 78, 82, 84, 85
Addams, Thomas 2
Advocacy 122
Agapes 10
Aggressive casework 113
Aid to (Families with) Dependent Children 3, 99, 105-106
Alexander, Cecil Frances 26
Alisky, Saul 122
Alternatives, to present programs 120, 134
Altemyer, Arthur 98
Ambrose 1, 13, 15, 17, 78, 97
American Civil Liberties Union 119
Analytic psychology 114, 115
Aptekar, Herbert 26
Aquinas, Thomas 15, 17-18, 97
Association for Improving the Condition of the Poor 72, 75-76
Augustine 16
Augustus, John 77
Authority, of social worker 105-106

B
Badges, worn by paupers 38
Bagdikian, Ben 117
Baldwin, Joseph 106
Barnett, Samuel 78
Barry, F. R. 65
Barton, Clara 77
Basil 12
Begging 21-22
Behavior and law 99
Behavior and love 147
Benedict, Ruth 101
Berdyaev, Nicolai 52, 66
Bernstein, Paul 93
Biestek, Felix 83, 84, 93, 95, 116

Bismark, Otto von 23, 96
Bisno, Herbert 64, 103
Black death, the 2
Booth, William 74-75
Bowers, Swithun 92
Bowie, Walter Russell 2
Brace, Charles Loring 74-75, 77
Breckenridge, Sophonisba 3
Brockway, Zebulon 77
Brown, Norman O. 89-90
Buber, Martin 53, 90

C
Calvin, John 35
Capitalist-Puritan religion 36, 40-43, 62-63, 146
Carter, Jimmy 135
Cash, Johnny 13
Chalmers, Thomas 2-3, 37-38, 46-48, 51, 61, 73
Chain of being, the 8
Charity 7, 8, 9, 16, 17-18, 20
Charity, indiscriminate 75-76
Charity Organization Society 75, 77, 115
Cheating 15, 19, 99, 133-344
Christian Socialists, the 20, 72-73
Christians, influx into social work 147
Christians, kinds of 147-148
Chrysostom 1, 13-15, 24
Church, as advocate for unpopular 18
Churchwardens 23
Clement of Alexandria 13
Client revolt, the 117-118
Cobden, Richard 43
Communism 64
Community Action Program 122
Confidentiality 99
Constitution of the Apostles, the 27
Control 9, 40-41, 77-78, 108, 109
Control, humanism and 64-65
Corn Laws 43
Covenant theology 33, 34
Culture, the 8, 82, 101, 116, 126

Cyprian 16

D
Davis, Allen F. 67-68, 71-72
Davis, Annie Lee 105
De Forest, Robert 77
De Paul, Vincent 20
De Schweinitz, Karl 3, 99, 105
Debs, Eugene 82
Defoe, Daniel 25
Demogrants 128-129
Denmark 38
Dennison, Edward 72
Depression, the 89, 95, 113
Devine, Edward 77
Determinism 92, 94, 95
Dewey, John 64, 69
Diagnostic school of social work 91, 101, 102
Dignity of individual 46, 95, 116, 128,
Direction, change in 3-4
Discipline 42, 77
Dix, Dorothea 77
Douglas, Paul 25
Due process 71, 96

E
Eddy, Thomas 77
Eisman, Martin 116
Election 32-33
Enclosure Acts 2, 21
Environment, as cause of poverty 68-69, 71-72, 77
Ericson, Erik 124
Equality 11-12
Esping-Andersen, Gosta 134
Evangelicism 42-45
Existentialism 114
External view of persons 90

F
Faatz, Anita 121
Falwell, Jerry 2, 34

Family allowances 114, 144
Feudal system 21
Fischer, Joel 124-125
Food stamps 119, 129, 130-132
Francis, of Assissi 16
Fraud squads 100
Freud, Sigmund 5, 50, 62, 89-91
Friendly visiting 20, 72-75
Fromm, Erich 50, 53-54
Frontier economy 32
Functional school of social work 91, 101

G
Genital character 50
George, Henry 78
Gilder, George 133-134 144
Gnostics, modern 35-36
Golden Rule, the 6
Goodwill 15
Government, as advocate 19
Government, as protector of property 42
Government, as employer 131
Grace, 36, 114
Grace and worldly success 34
Grace, Christians of 148
Great commandment, the 10
Greek civilization 7
Gregory of Nanianzen 13

H
Halmos, Paul 62, 121
Hamilton, Gordon 91, 92, 101, 102
Haammurabi 6
Harrington, Michael 117
Hartley, R. M. 73
Health insurance 130
Hill, Octavia 73
Hillman, Sydney 69
Hoey, Jane 100
Hollis, E. V. and A. L. Taylor 97
Hollis, Florence 92-93, 121

Residence requirements 119 (see also Settement Act)
Resistance to taking help 106
Responsibility for poor 7-8, 9-10, 105
Reynolds, Bertha 92, 102
Richmond, Mary 51, 79-82, 92
Ridley, Bishop 2
Right to assistance 52, 97
Right to assistance, attack on 105-106, 109-110
Rights 6, 17, 116, 127
Rights, erosion of 113-127
Riis, Jacob 77
Robinson, Virginia 91
Robertson, H. M. 91
Rome 1, 7
Rousseau, Jean-Jacques 79

S
Safty net 131-132
Salomon, Elizabeth 124
Saints, intolerable rule of 46, 135, 148
Salvation Army 74-75
Salzberger, Ronald 126
Sayers, Dorothy 57
Schor, Alvin 116, 123
Science 46, 49-54, 68, 70, 76, 89-90, 101-102, 113-114
Second Coming 12
Self-determination 81, 92-95, 126
Self-fulfillment 7, 9, 16, 45
Services 103-104, 117, 119-120
Shaftesbury, Lord 43
Shepherd of Hermas, the 15
Simon, William 130
Simons, Ronald 126
Sin 33, 41, 44-45, 57, 78-79
Skinner, B. F. 9
Smalley, Ruth 101
Smith, A. Delafield 98-99
Smith, Adam 38
Smylie, James H. 25
Social casework 80, 82, 95, 101, 121-123, 124-126
Social Darwinism 6, 54